The Dynamics of the Industrial Revolution

The Dynamics of the Industrial Revolution

Allan Thompson

Senior Lecturer in Economic History,
University of Melbourne

Edward Arnold

© Allan Thompson 1973

First published 1973
by Edward Arnold (Publishers) Ltd.,
25 Hill Street, London WIX 8LL

ISBN: 0 7131 5684 8

Printed in Great Britain by
Billing & Sons Limited, Guildford and London

Contents

Acknowledgements

I am deeply grateful for the help I have received from discussions with a number of my colleagues in the Faculty of Economics and Commerce, University of Melbourne. I am particularly indebted to Professor Geoffrey Blainey and Dr. Peter Drake for their guidance and invaluable comments. Similarly, I have received much help from the comments of Dr. Keith Trace, Monash University, and Dr. R. Max Hartwell, Nuffield College, Oxford.

My wife, Adele, has constantly encouraged me in word and deed, typing innumerable drafts and assisting in the preparation of the final typescript. Mrs. Helen Ferber sub-edited the final draft with great skill and admirable diplomacy.

If I have sometimes remained obdurate in the face of the wisdom and patience of these people, it is no fault of theirs.

Introduction

This study has its origins in the problems of teaching the history of the British industrial revolution to undergraduates. On this subject there is no difficulty in finding a series of topics which individually have great merit as intellectual exercises: the difficulty is that they are a series of disjointed topics. I have found it impossible to develop a broad theme which alone can make the subject obviously worthy of study. No matter how much we try to disguise the fact, we examine the individual topics by asking limited questions which vary little from topic to topic: was this factor *the* prime cause of the industrial revolution? was it indispensable? Our difficulty is that the answer to the first question is always (or should be) no, and to the second always (or nearly always) yes. Sooner of later it becomes obvious that the questions are only partly relevant to an explanation of how and why the industrial revolution occurred. The effect is to assemble a long list of indispensables which we seem unable to fit together—we do not produce a historical mechanism of change using all the assembled pieces.

The result of the limited research horizons of economic historians is that their analyses of the industrial revolution lack cohesion and conviction. Syntheses are not quite respectable: they are undergraduate texts, or somewhat entertaining visions: they are not quite serious scholarship. The truth is that they cannot be more, because the topic researcher is indifferent to problems of syntheses and co-ordination: he pursues his topic in isolation. While this remains true there is little promise that economic history will further illuminate the great problems of industrialization. I believe that it can and should illuminate these problems; but to do so will require rethinking our research aims and approaches.

The first chapter of this book offers a general discussion of some basic problems of approach to economic development issues. The second discusses the term 'industrial revolution' and sketches British economic growth in the modern era. The next six chapters consist of a series of essays about particular aspects of British industrial revolution studies written in the context of the earlier general discussion. These chapters are an effort to discuss the problems of studying disparate topics so that they are truly part of a broad theme: they should be seen as variations on the theme outlined in the first chapter. In short, I have tried to discover why existing studies fail to produce work that can be synthesized, and have explored the problems of producing such work; and the book offers some tentative solutions for solving these problems. At another level I have put forward criticisms of existing industrial revolution studies on these three broad fronts:

(1) that cultural and social factors are neglected;
(2) that far too little cognizance is taken of interactions between factors involved in industrialization;
(3) that treatment of chronology is weak, partly perhaps because it is widely—though wrongly—regarded as comparatively unimportant.

This is not to argue that all historians neglect social and cultural factors, interactions or chronology. The work of Tawney, Ashton, Habakkuk, Tucker, Deane and Cole and many other fine historians would quickly give the lie to that proposition. Nevertheless, as I hope the book will demonstrate, the three deficiencies are sufficiently general to be of major concern to economic history. The balance of attention to each of these three broad issues differs from chapter to chapter in this book; but each is important to most industrial revolution topics.

The three deficiencies may be interconnected. For example, one of the reasons for the neglect of social factors may be the difficulty of dealing with continuing interaction between social and economic factors.

Note: Works listed in the Select Bibliography at the end of the book are referred to in footnotes by author's name and date of publication only. Publication details of works listed in the Further Reading list at the end of each chapter are given in the Select Bibliography.

1 Interrelations in Economic Development

The academic world still does not understand industrialization. Economic historians' accounts of past industrializations are diffuse and unconvincing: economists' plans for developing countries do not live up to their promises. In important respects these weaknesses have similar causes.

Industrialization is of course a very long-term process, stretching over a much longer time-span than most modern economic analyses. In such a context some of the simplifying assumptions of economists are suspect. These include assumptions that social institutions, intellectual abilities and ethics or value systems, are unchanging during the period of analysis. These things do change over time, and such changes are an integral part of industrialization—at least for 'traditional' societies.

Some economists, for example W. A. Lewis,[1] have recognized the importance of social influences. But economists are still reluctant to accept the full implications of these general works for their functional models. The cultural factors pose particularly intractable analytical problems, but to ignore them often makes the economic analysis wrong or irrelevant.

Thus economists are prone to explain the rate of labour-saving innovation by analysing the relative cost movements of capital and labour. This kind of analysis may be applied satisfactorily to relatively short-run fluctuations, but may be quite misleading for longer-run movements. Other determinants may have much more influence upon innovation in the long run. For instance, we know that attitudes towards machine breaking (and automation) have varied greatly in the past, and the comparative history of, say, France and Britain in the late eighteenth century suggests that these attitudes may determine the commercial success of an innovation. Also, in the very long run, the *capacity* to invent and to make commercial innovations varies for many reasons. Inventive and innovative ability will obviously vary with the ability to solve new technical problems. In turn, the ability to solve problems depends upon the quality of intellectual skills available:

[1] W. Arthur Lewis, 1955.

it depends upon an inventive scientific elite. Capacity to innovate also depends upon the ability of a large cross-section of the workforce to build and maintain increasingly complex equipment, and perhaps in some fields upon an increasing ability to operate complex equipment. These technical abilities rest, of course, upon the overall educational standards of the community.

Moreover, being a risk-taking venture, innovation requires more than the technical ability to solve new problems. We know well enough that willingness to take risks varies between individuals and between communities. In the long run, changes in willingness to take commercial risks may be amongst the prime determinants of changes in innovation rates. Willingness to undertake risk is in turn determined by a range of complex factors. These include the motives of entrepreneurs—which may originate in the aspirations which their society sanctions. For instance, social influences may determine the intensity of the desire of entrepreneurs for profit, wealth and 'success', and also what they may do with their entrepreneurial power, such as providing work for their kin. Here we are inevitably drawn into questions of what determines whether one society is individualistic and materialistic compared with another. It is simple delusion to suppose that variations in individualism and materialism are not major determinants of risk-taking proclivities.

Further, community attitudes can influence the actual riskiness of a venture. This is most obviously true of the law. The law must protect property and contract, and ultimately community attitudes decide whether (or to what extent) they are protected. Community attitudes also impose constraints upon the methods used by a businessman, thus varying the risk he takes in trying to achieve his objectives. Guild or union regulation of prices, standards, and labour entry illustrate this point. Political stability and monetary stability also determine his risk, and these depend upon the political maturity of the community and upon attitudes towards, and understanding of (amongst other things), the functions of money and monetary institutions.

Enough has been said to illustrate my point that the social and cultural background to the economy is a vital determinant of how it works, and that changes in these things unquestionably influence changes in the rate of economic progress. The question is not whether social and cultural factors are important, but how to study them in order to fit them into a functional economic analysis.

Economists concerned with the pragmatic problems of specific development projects are more likely than theoretical economists to recognize the importance of social factors, since experience has shown that the best economic projects are useless if the local people oppose them for cultural reasons.[2] More and more economists are aware that a project must be carefully planned in its social context, although they are as yet clearly far from doing so with complete success. Often the cultural obstacles to change are tackled by economic aid missions which achieve some progress after considerable effort, only to discover later that the local people often lapse into old ways soon after the aid mission withdraws.[3] This may indicate that the obstacles are more complex than we realize.

Moreover, the interest of the pragmatic economist is basically short-term: what can be done in the next five years given local resources, attitudes and institutions? While it is a healthy sign that such questions are asked, it is really only a beginning—and I say this without wishing to denigrate this interesting work. For some problems this is probably the most fruitful approach, but there are long-term issues which we cannot afford to ignore. These issues revolve around the problem of structuring development: of dovetailing or integrating the various sectorial changes to achieve a reasonably efficient pattern of development. In saying this I assume that it is not feasible to do everything that could be done. There will be resource limits which involve priority choices. Should we concentrate on domestic industry for a time, or heavy industry, factory production, agriculture, education? In order to make priority choices we need some dynamic pattern of development in mind. This of course is an over-simplification. Development plans do not require a choice between one or the other of these things but a blending of each. Education cannot be neglected any more than agriculture or industry. The problem, however, is still one of priority choices: how much effort in each direction is required? What sort of development pattern is anticipated and what inputs of various kinds are necessary for this purpose?

Furthermore, patterns are obviously necessary (a) where some factors have a long gestation period—education is the most obvious example here—and (b) because some economic changes have a complex social background, and the pace of economic change is often determined by the pattern of social change. We must avoid making wasteful plans which simply will not work for cultural reasons.

The problem of integration requires much deeper knowledge of interactions than is required for a limited specific project. Thus, for instance, it is said that success in agricultural reform in Mexico has hardened the old village structure and made overall modernization *more* difficult.[4] Moreover, economists are inclined to note cultural

[2] For example C. Geerts, 1956; R. Firth, 1963; W. R. Goldschmidt, 1952; Mya Maung, 1964.
[3] H. Leibenstein, 1966b.   [4] B. F. Hoselitz, 1952–3.

differences but still plan on the assumption that these differences will not markedly affect the plan—perhaps assuming that cultural resistance can be broken down. Thus they may observe that the class system in India tends to break down under stress. But what happens while the breakdown is proceeding? How long will it take? What is the cause of the breakdown? How are economic plans to be modified during the transition? Economists are often misled by the ease of initial penetration of commercialization into traditional societies. This can often be achieved without changing the fundamental basis of the society. There is still a huge gap between these beginnings and the creation of a fully commercialized industrial society.

There is also another dimension to be considered: we have been talking mainly of the direct constraints of a social system on economic change; but there are connections in the opposite direction which may also lead to serious social and economic problems. If economic change is so rapid that it causes the old authority structure to collapse before a new one can be established, the result may be a social anarchy and economic devastation. The unforeseen consequences of 'development' may well be a major cause of the social unrest in the Third World, not just in the cities but also in the countryside. To continue to regard these interplays as economically irrelevant is to court social disaster and economic failure. In summary, it appears that economists are not yet taking sufficient account of the cultural context of economic change. The same can be said of economic historians.

Why have economists and historians neglected the social context of economic change and the problems of integrated patterns of growth? Perhaps it is simply a conscious or unconscious recognition of how enormously complicated functional models would be if the social influences were included. A great increase in complexity would result, not just because many more variables would be added but also because the relationships between the variables are highly complex, and particularly because the relationships frequently include feedbacks or mutual interactions. Mutual interactions are at the heart of our difficulties. Not only do social changes affect the working of the economy, but changes in the economy affect social changes and various aspects of social change interact on each other.

For instance, social attitudes can influence the number of men prepared to become industrial enterpreneurs as well as the methods and motives of their operations. But the number will also be determined by long-term economic expectations which are partly a product of past economic performance. Moreover, attitudes (such as religious attitudes to great wealth) can alter as the economy alters. In a stagnant economy social stability requires an ethic which frowns upon rapid accumulation' of wealth, because rapid accumulation must usually be at the expense of other people. A peasant agrarian society, for instance, may disapprove of individual initiative in order to maintain social stability.[5] But such an ethic is put under pressure where economic growth can allow a man to accumulate wealth without robbing others, and indeed may allow him to provide more work and wealth for others. If ethics change as a result of changing circumstances, this will alter the conditions upon which the economy works.

Economic changes (and expectations) are also affected by other variables—population growth, the nature of demand, the responsiveness of the agricultural sector; these in turn are influenced by attitudes towards family limitation, age of marriage, laws of inheritance, the class system, attitudes towards a money economy, and so on. Thus the complexity of social and economic change arises from the way in which many factors influence others and are in turn influenced by changes in them: there is mutual interaction.

Existing studies of cultural influences upon the economy tend to ignore these mutual interactions, and *because of this they are not dynamic*: they do not explain the total mechanism of economic change. Thus we have some interesting work (often by sociologists and anthropologists) on cultural obstacles to economic development[6] which nevertheless skirts the dynamic issues. Ayal[7] shows that Japanese social values were more conducive to industrialization than Thai social values—but how did they come to be more conducive? What influenced the differences, and over what time-span? This is not to deny the value of studies which clarify and define the ways in which social factors influence the economy; but the point is that they are only a partial help. We need to know how social and economic changes are produced in a situation of mutual interaction if we are to analyse the *dynamics* of economic development.

These remarks illustrate why the pragmatic approach of the economists may not work well for some problems even in the short run. They may assume, for example, that a management training scheme can solve entrepreneurial problems, when in fact entrepreneurial attitudes and performance may be inextricably interwoven with social attitudes, beliefs and habits. The creation of an entrepreneurial class may be a complex problem of social interconnections, not a simple question of training in managerial skills.

Economic historians do no better than economists or sociologists

---

[5] W. R. Goldschmidt, 1952.

[6] See, for example, the special issue of *Human Organization*, 'Contours of Culture Change in South Asia', Vol. 22 (1963).

[7] E. B. Ayal, 1963.

in dealing with interactions. Many historical studies look at a particular factor to see whether it was indispensable to the industrial revolution—and nearly always discover that it was: because economic growth could not have been as rapid in the absence of population growth, or the expansion of trade, or the agrarian or scientific revolutions, and so on. But few of these studies maintain a balance by examining the interactions from the other direction: the effects of economic growth upon the particular factor studied. Historians have found, for example, that British entrepreneurs were usually daring and resourceful compared with their Continental counterparts in the eighteenth century. They conclude that the existence of these men was an important reason why British economic growth was so high.[8] And so it was; but we must ask equally whether the pressures and opportunities created by economic growth were not largely responsible for the characteristics of British entrepreneurs. The typical historian is a topic specialist whose research technique revolves around a narrow concern to demonstrate the importance of his topic—he is a 'topic introvert' and ignores mutual interactions.

The economic historian is undoubtedly aware that such interactions are involved, but as we shall see, he tends to return to linear causation patterns which must necessarily short-circuit some of the continuing interactions. It is my purpose to analyse the weaknesses of current industrialization histories more closely and suggest an alternative approach. It is time that historians dispensed with their topic introversion and with the pursuit of single causes and simple lines of causation. This not only produces bad history: it is the reason why economists find so little instruction in the work of historians.

The weakness of economic historians in dealing with interrelations can be illustrated by examining syntheses of the British industrial revolution. Many general accounts of the industrial revolution are not syntheses at all, but merely a collection of essays on various aspects of British society before and during the industrial revolution. More serious analytical efforts are normally based on linear causation patterns in which chronology is inadequately established. Thus we see two historians finding that in industry, agriculture and transport, innovation was 'stimulated by the great upsurge of population which began a generation before',[9] but another finding that population growth was the *result* of two decades of good harvests after 1730, and later of improved farming methods, together with the growing demand for labour.[10] Examples of disagreements of this kind can be so multiplied that the

[8] B. F. Hoselitz, 1955; C. Wilson, 1955.
[9] Phyllis Deane and W. A. Cole, 1962.
[10] R. M. Hartwell, 1965a, p. 10.

possible number of hypothetical models is almost infinite. Similar weaknesses are also apparent in the lengthening lists of revolutions—perhaps five or six agricultural revolutions in Britain (see Chapter 3), as well as numerous industrial revolutions.[11] Here the weakness lies in providing standards of comparison between various phases of growth.

Moreover, the synthesizers seldom attempt to fit the non-economic factors into the mechanism despite a long acquaintance with some, notably the Protestant ethic. Non-economic factors are sometimes said to have provided a favourable (or unfavourable) environment for industrialization, but the mechanics of the changing relationship between economic and non-economic factors are usually ignored.

Not all synthesizers can be accused of all of these faults, as we can see, for instance, in the work of T. S. Ashton and Paul Mantoux.[12] But even the best syntheses lack functional analysis of the continuing interactions between social and economic factors in the periods leading up to, and during, the industrial revolution.

More important, the synthesizers are constrained by the limitations of their raw material: it is principally the basic research upon which they draw which is at fault. More especially the fault lies in historical methods of research, which ignore the implications of interaction. It is essentially the result of the topic introversion of the historical researcher. Most historians would probably openly acknowledge the importance of comparative chronology, of the relationships between social, cultural and economic factors and of mutual interaction, but in practice they frequently ignore them when formulating their research hypotheses. At the topic research level they fail to ask themselves whether their questions and methods will produce findings which can be incorporated into a cohesive explanation of the industrial revolution. Their retort might be that historians cannot agree on an appropriate technique for dealing with the problems of interaction and in the meantime research must continue. Yet no historian should allow himself to ignore the broader implications of his work. For those who aspire to be more than antiquarian, some broad theme must underlie the study of all topics and sub-topics. If this is not so, then the study is often pointless, dominated by the material available rather than by truly intellectual problems. If our methods and procedures do not elucidate the theme of our subject this is a matter of concern, not only for a few methodologists, but for all involved in the subject.

[11] See D. C. Coleman, 1956.
[12] T. S. Ashton, 1968; P. Mantoux, 1961.

ON SIMPLIFYING THE COMPLEX

Historians' topic introversion has led to the proliferation of factors 'indispensable' to industrial growth. The literature abounds with factors which some eminent historian has shown to be essential to the industrial revolution—with what Hirschman calls 'an ever lengthening list of factors and conditions, of obstacles and prerequisites'.[13] The problem then is to explain how all these indispensables come to appear more or less simultaneously.

In struggling with this problem historians are in effect struggling with the whole complex problem of interactions between the various factors, though they do not always seem to be aware of this. Indeed, the very idea of a large number of 'indispensables' is often subconsciously sidestepped by historians when they emphasize one factor as the 'main factor' or 'prime mover' in the industrial revolution. This brings us to the second major family of research questions: was x or y a prime mover? Most would recognize that one factor cannot be a prime mover in the Aristotelian sense of being something from which all else follows; we know that a number of factors may be necessary, but no one factor is both necessary and sufficient. Nevertheless, the tendency to emphasize one particular factor has an almost irresistible attraction for historians. One must assume that they do not continue to make the same elementary error, but alternative meanings of these ubiquitous phrases are never explained or even explored.

What exactly do historians mean when they talk about prime movers, engines of growth and the main factor? If they mean only that this particular factor was one of the indispensables to industrialization one could not quarrel, but the usage plainly goes beyond this, since one factor is elevated above all others, though usually in very guarded terms. Perhaps the historian is trying to establish an order of importance for the various factors. However, if it is admitted that there were a number of changes in society and the economy which were all necessary, what does an order of importance mean? If x is indispensable, what is the significance of saying y is more important? In any case, an order of importance can only be established on some specific criterion. What is the criterion?

One criterion often used is whether a particular factor was the most significant stimulus to growth in a particular period. There can be no doubt that there were historically important stimuli to economic growth, such as the growth of foreign trade in eighteenth-century Britain. However, though they are obviously part of an explanation of the

[13] A. O. Hirschman, 1961, p. 1.

industrial revolution, one may doubt whether they are central to the explanation. A stimulus may initiate growth, but this need not lead to industrialization—which involves long-term growth, not just a boom. It is the *reactions* to the boom conditions which determine whether it continues or peters out. The reactions are likely to be determined by the general economic and social setting in which the stimulus is felt, rather than by the nature of the initial stimulus itself. Since it is the response which is of central importance, the stimulus has not deserved the emphasis which has often been given. It is true that the point can be taken too far, because certain aspects of the stimulus may be important. For instance, the *way* in which British foreign trade grew in the eighteenth century was significant in determining how the cotton industry developed. Nevertheless, trade expansion cannot fully explain the industrial revolution: because the reactions to the opportunities created by trade expansion were determined by many social and economic factors.

It must be admitted that some attempts have been made to analyse interactions—for example, between population growth and agricultural improvement in the eighteenth century. Unfortunately in the final analysis this is only slightly better than looking for the initial stimulus, and this is so for two major reasons. Firstly, the method used has generally been crude. *A priori* analysis is used to demonstrate that interaction between the two is both possible and highly likely. Typically, an attempt is then made to show which is likely to be the controlling or stronger factor, usually by showing which came first chronologically. This means, of course, that analysis of continuing interaction is precluded. It also means that the approach turns out to be only a variant of the 'initial stimulus' approach.

Secondly, the analysis is generally confined to two variables. It is therefore inadequate because it fails to include mutual interactions with other factors which were admitted to be indispensable. Thus population growth may have stimulated agricultural change in the eighteenth century, but how far would change have proceeded without parliamentary enclosure? The transition from government opposition to government enforcement of enclosure was not simply a product of population growth and agricultural revolution in the eighteenth century.

The inadequacies of this two-variant approach are equally obvious when we begin to ask some simple subsidiary questions about the relationships. Why should population growth in the eighteenth century have changed agriculture so much, when the rate and duration of population growth were not unique or perhaps even remarkable up to the time when agriculture began to respond? We do not have to delve far into such questions to realize that the two-factor analysis is inadequate, and it becomes clear that the relationship between agriculture and population—important though it may have been—must be explained in a wider context, a context of interactions between a number of social, intellectual and economic variables.

Some historians are aware that the fragmentation of British studies has become serious. Their work does not seem to have had much impact on the profession, however, perhaps partly because their solutions are indefinite. For example, R. M. Hartwell proposes an approach which leans upon the techniques of development economics. He writes that a full explanation of British growth requires us to 'describe the economy before industrialization, analyse its structural relationships, and identify its internal constraints'.[14] It is of course the absence of any analysis of the 'structural relationships' which has been the chief lacuna in the past, and Hartwell suggests that we should look to economists' growth models and techniques for inspiration.[15] Obviously economic historians must be prepared to learn from economics, but they will not learn much from economic development theory in its present condition. Specifically, as we have already said, economists have not yet included as functional elements a large number of factors, particularly social factors, which seem to influence economic performance profoundly. That they have not done so is partly because quantification of some important social influences is not yet possible even in ideal circumstances. Furthermore, the kind of approach which Hartwell suggests requires more precise and comprehensive quantification than the economist or historian can command. Can we look forward, for example, to measuring the *extent* to which 'an increase in population for non-economic reasons promoted economic growth'[16] in eighteenth-century Britain? The methodology for carrying out this measurement is not explained to us. It may be possible to estimate the influence of population growth upon economic growth by regression analysis, but can we estimate the extent to which population growth was caused by non-economic factors, and is it possible to combine the two answers? If we find that population growth was partially economically induced, our regression analysis loses the meaning we gave it because there is a definite, if partial, relationship between the two in both directions.[17]

Furthermore, there seems to be a fundamental weakness in regression and lag analysis for very long-term problems. Thus time-series analysis can tell us whether there is a (statistical) relationship between two

[14] R. M. Hartwell, 1965b, p. 171.
[15] *Ibid.*, p. 172.
[16] *Ibid.*, p. 171.
[17] J. D. Gould (1969) has lucidly explained the difficulties of the counterfactual approach to economic problems which are 'open' to influences from non-economic factors.

variables, but it cannot tell us whether it is a two-way relationship. Nevertheless, if we prove or assume that there was a two-way relationship, lag analysis can tell us which of the two led the way. However, in doing this it is merely demonstrating a chronological leadership which does not necessarily tell us which is the dominant partner in the long run—and this is a fundamental weakness in the technique for our purpose. Suppose, for instance, that lag analysis shows that growth of the number of entrepreneurs always preceded shifts in religious attitudes towards business and businessmen: that religion accommodated itself to change in the nature of the community. We should not then ignore religious attitudes on the assumption that they are merely passive. The *speed* at which religious attitudes adjust may be the *decisive limitation* on economic growth in the long run.

Similarly, lag analysis may show that the growth of the economy determines short-run fluctuations of technological innovations, but it must be obvious that in the long run the state of effective technology partly depends upon the technical abilities of the community. Therefore in the long run technical abilities must be a *potential restraint* upon the rate of innovation. Lag analysis cannot show whether technical ability was acting as a restraint. Of course, if it acted as a restraint it must be a highly important aspect of industrialization, and we will obviously want to explain what influences were at work upon it. Furthermore, even if we could definitely say that it was not an actual restraint[18] it is still essential to explain why it was not. Why were the British capable of producing technical inventions on an unprecedented scale? Clearly it was not only because of sudden economic opportunity. It is just as necessary to explain why potential restraining factors did not operate historically as it is to explain why some did operate. Brinley Thomas's lag analysis of migration and investment showed that investment lagged behind migration in U.S.A. between 1840 and 1870.[19] No one would be so foolish as to conclude therefore that investment was unimportant in the growth of the U.S.A. at this time, or that migration was the only important influence upon investment. We must not be misled into disregard of the lagging variable in other cases simply because the lagging variable is less obviously important than investment.

The point may be further illustrated by reference to Deane and Cole's

[18] I ignore the question of whether it would be *feasible* to support such a conclusion. To do so one would need to show that a higher rate of technical improvement would not have brought faster economic growth. In the very long period this is highly unlikely, so we are led to the conclusion that in some sense technical change must be a restraining influence. The point is that it may never be possible to establish either case.

[19] B. Thomas, *Migration and Economic Growth* (Cambridge University Press, London, 1954), Ch. 7.

interesting analysis of the role of foreign trade in eighteenth-century Britain.[20] They demonstrate the great dependence of the West Indies, the Americas and West Africa upon British markets. This complements earlier work which emphasized that British exports were increasingly and massively dependent on these same areas.[21] Obviously, therefore, it is possible that either British or American growth could have stimulated the mutual exchange of goods between the two areas. On this assumption Deane and Cole then apply a version of lag analysis to show which was the exogenous stimulant. However, this technique is not satisfactory for long-run analysis because in the long run the lagging variable may restrain growth, i.e. determine the rate of growth. Thus, even if we were sure that British demand set the pace of trade growth in the short run, in the long run the pace of trade growth may have been determined by how readily and effectively American producers responded to the opportunities of an expanding British demand for their products. It was only possible for the Americans to respond in the way that they did because they had ready access to fertile land (comparatively free of previous inhabitants), a tradition of commercial agricultural production and import of manufactures, rapidly growing population and so on. The point is that lag analysis does not allow us to say that a lagging variable can be ignored in explaining development rates.

All this is not to say that econometric techniques are useless in industrial studies. Indeed, they have a great potential for removing empirical woolliness—for disposing of the kind of methodology which allows us to find half a dozen agricultural revolutions in Britain. I believe that this kind of woolliness is more pervasive and important than is sometimes realized; but here the main point is that it is distinct from the problem of developing adequate methods for dealing with the complex interactions in a developing economy. Improvement in empirical knowledge does not necessarily improve our ability to explain interactions. An econometric approach may be useful for some features of our studies, particularly where the problems of comparison are important, but we cannot assume that econometric studies will slot nicely into the overall subject. Their results *may be* just as intractable as those of present historical studies. We are still left with the highly important and inescapable problem of explaining the interrelationships in this complex process of development.

Rostow has a quite different approach.[22] At first sight his emphasis on pre-conditions does seem to illuminate the problem of interrelations.

[20] Phyllis Deane and W. A. Cole, 1962, esp. pp. 80–88.
[21] *Ibid.*, p. 28. They describe trade as 'strategically important' to British growth but in subsequent analysis clearly decide that it was a dependent variable.
[22] W. W. Rostow, 1960.

He is arguing that rapid growth (the take-off) depends upon the prior establishment of certain characteristics in the society and that society will continue to change as growth continues. One may argue, however, that this does little more than emphasize that there *are* interrelationships, and that it does not offer a way of analysing these relationships in a dynamic way. Above all, despite appearances to the contrary, Rostow's is a static model in the sense that it relates conditioning *only* to a particular point of time. How does agriculture get to the state that he says it must reach at take-off? What factors influence the agricultural community as it moves towards this 'conditioned' state? He offers no way of dealing analytically with the continuous changes in relationships which are the essential characteristic of transition.

One way of expressing the problem of interrelatedness is to say that many of the conditions and elements which are essential to the process of growth are themselves influenced by growth. Hartwell makes this point[23] and Habakkuk[24] develops it further. Habakkuk writes that most of the factors which have been said to be *pre-conditions* prove to be essentially manifestations of growth. In this he is probably following Hirschman, who says: 'while we are at first discouraged by the long list of resources and circumstances whose presence has been shown to be needed for economic development, we now find that these resources and circumstances are not so scarce or so difficult to realise, *provided however, that economic development itself first raises its head.*'[25]

Here is an appealing proposition: that growth will call forth most of the elements of a modern society. Its appeal is reinforced by the knowledge that growth *tends* to lead attitudes and institutions towards tolerance of new requirements. Superficially it appears, therefore, that maintaining maximum growth will be the best road to social change. Consequently much of Hirschman's analysis is concerned with maximizing incentives for growth, by taking account of linkages between one industry and another.

However, this approach skirts the vital problem of comparative timing. The elements which are basic to a modern economy are surely *produced at different speeds.* For instance, industrial entrepreneurs may emerge quickly if there is already a substantial merchant class; it may take much more time to mould a stable urban factory workforce from a traditional agrarian community.

Hirschman is aware that problems of timing exist, but apparently believes that *ad hoc* responses to the pressures created by growth are the best means of dealing with timing problems: 'Thus they [under-

[23] R. M. Hartwell, 1965b, p. 180.
[24] H. J. Habakkuk, 1965a, p. 118.
[25] A. O. Hirschman, 1961, p. 5.

developed countries] will find out about the changes required in their own society in the course of the development process as they make false starts and as they meet with, and overcome, successive obstacles.'[26] However, I believe that such a policy would only be sensible if we assumed that incentives would be so strong that problems would be steamrollered: that action would be immediate and almost instantly effective. Such assumptions are obviously unrealistic. Economic performance is often determined by non-economic elements, such as religious values, which are very imperfectly responsive to economic incentives. Moreover, some economic and social elements have a long build-up period as well as a long fruition period. Thus it is a commonplace that educational expansion must be cumulative to some extent. Consequently educational reform may only be effective over a long period; it may be highly dangerous to delay the beginning of reform until the need is overwhelming. Shortage of educated workers may stifle growth before the backlog of education can be overcome.

Hirschman also has interesting accounts of social and institutional impediments to effective entrepreneurship and management, and has other references to what he calls 'forces corroding development'.[27] These are obvious qualifications to his basic model, but precisely how do they qualify it? Hirschman's answer would be perhaps that social and other impediments are *bottlenecks*. However, if this were meant to imply that they are mainly dependent variables which cannot jeopardize growth or alter the mechanics of change, but can only slow or delay it, then he would clearly be wrong. Experience has shown that local peoples have often consciously or unconsciously rejected development projects for cultural reasons.[28] Thus the economic pressures which are supposed to change social attitudes may never do so—precisely because of social resistance. Cultural beliefs and habits may also modify economic performance even when a project is not totally rejected. Beliefs and habits may change very slowly indeed, and an economic plan must try to take account of this, fitting its sequences around the timing of the slowest-moving links in the chain of causation. It is during transition that institutions and values carefully formulated to maintain a stagnant society must be modified to admit and encourage change, so that the whole community tolerates the social and economic instability which inevitably accompanies economic progress. It is not simply that the Indian peasant is ignorant, it is also that he often prefers the stability of his inherited life to the comparative turmoil implied in new methods of production which may alter his way of life. Many 'five year plans'

[26] A. O. Hirschman, 1961, p. 10; see also p. 64.
[27] *Ibid.*, pp. 11–24, 44 ff., 78–83. See also his stimulating little article, 1965.
[28] See footnote 3 above.

have foundered on ignorance of this simple but fundamental fact, which may well be the underlying difference between an 'abortive industrial surge' and a 'take-off'.

The danger of the Hirschman approach is that it may cause policy to be misdirected. The policy-maker must make sure that the potential frustrations to growth are influenced as early as possible—perhaps even before modernization begins. Moreover, concentrating resources on modernization may actually minimize pressures for change upon slow-moving factors. For example, agricultural change may involve major social reconstruction, so that agriculture will respond very slowly. Consequently it may be a mistake to devote too much effort to modernization of industry; the modern sector will be limited in size and accordingly pressure upon the agricultural sector may be highly selective. In the long run it may be quicker and more efficient to adopt a policy designed to put pressure for change on the widest possible cross-section of the agricultural community in the early stages of growth—perhaps by a policy of developing traditional industries. broad + base

I do not mean that modern industry should be excluded from early plans; but it is clear in the long run that the main problem is to dovetail changes in a number of different economic and cultural factors. Hirschman mentions efficient sequences, but whereas he appears to regard them as secondary problems, they seem to me by contrast to be *central* to successful planning. They are essentially problems of comparative timing. Hirschman's emphasis on *ad hoc* pressures as a timing device is very imperfect, and indeed could be dangerous. Moreover this device does not *solve* problems of priority—it simply delays them. Thus if the economist waits until pressures for education become irresistible he still faces questions of priority. How much education is needed now? How can we dovetail a programme of educational progress with the future needs of the expanding economy? These problems must be faced sooner or later, and it is better to face them early. No amount of waiting will cause them to disappear or even to shrink, but it *may* cause expansion to crumble.

MUTUAL CAUSATION

If we examine each of the 'solutions' to the problem of interrelations we can see a common thread. All are attempts in one way or another to establish a straight chain of causation. All are dominated by linear thought patterns, in which the object is to construct an explanation in terms of a series of variables linked to a controlling influence, either directly or through a straight chain of causation. This reasoning runs into two insoluble difficulties. First, the majority of factors must become dependent variables because the system is logically inconsistent if this is not so. Yet this cannot be reconciled with the fact that many so-called dependent variables may exert decisive influence upon the entire system. The linear causation approach is logically incapable of explaining why cultural factors may prevent or heavily retard industrialization, as is almost certainly true of India. Similarly, a solution must be capable of accounting for random influences on economic performance: the influence of great men upon the development of science or upon social ideology; chance events which determine whether a disastrous war occurs or not—or even the outcome of a war; or a country's access to raw materials suitable for exploiting a new production technique; and so on.

The second difficulty of a linear mode of thought is that it cannot deal with a situation of mutual interaction. Hence the dilemma of Hirschman, who so brilliantly expounds the potential influence of some social factors, but at the same time tries to retain the idea that most factors are linked to a central engine of growth. The truth is that any acceptable solution must allow for both the potentially decisive influence of a number of factors and a series of mutual and continuing interactions. which are which.

Only circular causation patterns are capable of incorporating these fundamental requirements—we *must* think in terms of two-way interdependence between a number of factors. Thus we may accept (with Hirschman) that economic growth will tend to alter social attitudes in the right direction, but at the same time we must acknowledge that the speed at which these attitudes change may be autonomously determined, for instance by the pronouncements of religious leaders. Therefore while attitudes may be conditioned by changing circumstance (economic growth) they may also be subject to independent influences, and may also determine the rate at which economic growth can proceed (by influencing the number of able entrepreneurs available, for example). Only a circular explanation pattern can make sense of the realities of this situation.

The effort to avoid circular or two-way interaction is like an attempt to explain the rising ownership of television receivers by pointing to falling prices: people are buying more because they are cheaper. While this is true, it is also true that they are cheaper partly because more people are buying them—making possible falling costs because of economies of scale. The rise in ownership in the long run is the result of a continuing interplay of rising sales and falling production costs. It is also not possible to dismiss one as purely a response to the movement of the other. External influences also play a part; fashion may influence the growth of sales, and such things as design of component parts the costs of production. A simple linear explanation of the rise of television ownership will simply not do.

This is not to deny that one aspect of the two sides of an interaction *may* have a dominating role; but it is unsafe to *assume* that either will have a dominating role, just as it is unsafe to assume that a particular pattern of dominance will be the same in all cases and for all time. For most factors it is not possible to establish dominance or dependence on purely theoretical grounds in a long-run situation. Moreover, as we have noted, in the long run a passive factor may be a decisive restraint upon growth rates.

A GUIDE TO PATTERNS OF GROWTH

However, while this may tell us what requirements a solution must meet, it does not tell us what solution is possible. It should be said at once that I see no immediate prospect of a theory which will at once meet these requirements and be amenable to empirical research. Nevertheless, there is, I believe, a useful substitute for such a theory. It is based on our observation that the Hirschman theory ignores the time factor, by ignoring both the way in which some factors respond slowly to change and the way in which random influences may cause quite different patterns of change in a particular factor in different circumstances.

What is required is some way of relating the various factors one to another in some consistent way. It is true that there is no fully satisfactory way of doing this, to give the kind of precision which the model-builders would like. My suggestion is a compromise which emphasizes time relationships. A time-chart of development would show all the factors which we believe were capable of influencing the pace of industrialization. We would produce a kind of historical-critical path analysis. The aim would be to show the time period over which these factors evolved. We would also seek to explain observed differences in time scales in terms of historical circumstances. Thus, for example, we may postulate that a fully industrialized society requires a commercialized agriculture—we may investigate the phases of the development of commercial agriculture in particular cases, and we may investigate historical circumstance to explain why the time span of a particular phase differed from case to case. In saying that this approach will not do all that economists would like done, we recognize the limitations of our capacities, and we also reflect the limitations of our material. Yet even if we are not in a position to deliver the Holy Grail, the substitute may be informative and suggestive. An integrated chronological history of the factors influencing industrialization, with an analysis of the influences upon this chronology, will be a valuable practical guide to what has altered during past industrializations, how much and at what stage it altered, what influenced the change, and whether it did so concurrently with or as a prelude to other changes. These are questions within the potential competence of historians and the time-chart approach.

What I propose is surely not new. Yet if historians claim that they are attempting to do these things, two points must be made. First, it is time that these aims were made explicit. It is fair to say that few development economists would understand exactly what economic historians are trying to achieve: what framework underlies their investigations, and what kind of explanations they hope to present in the course of time. Secondly, if students of British industrialization do try to answer such questions they are often far from doing so satisfactorily. In many cases the aim is lost in the detail of research projects. This often appears as an offhanded treatment of chronology—sometimes to the point where a whole work is devoted to explaining the causes and consequences of a 'movement' which is assumed rather than proved. The point can only be demonstrated by a detailed examination at particular topics, as we will do in subsequent chapters.

Of course there are practical difficulties. The proposition that it is possible to distinguish definite phases of social and economic readjustment may be repugnant to historians who see history as a 'seamless web'. They argue that it is impossible to understand an event in a vacuum—it can only be understood and explained by the way in which the community reacts to circumstances, and this reaction is conditioned by the traditions, the values, the institutions of society—that is, by its prior history. This is perfectly true, but at the same time it is surely crucial to any serious historical study that it be possible to distinguish phases in the evolution of social phenomena. Such phases are what academic scholarship is normally concerned to define, explore, and explain. Nevertheless, any historical phase is partly a product of the conditions at its beginning, and the conditions are a product of prior history. For instance, it would be foolish to overlook the comparative maturity of British agriculture before the agricultural revolution when analysing the how and why of that revolution. The same is true of many factors which we would investigate under a time-chart approach. This means that the timing of change only has meaning within the specific context involved.

It is also clear that change does not conveniently begin in the modern era: there was change before the classic agricultural revolution, and even the most timeless societies are not completely static. Therefore methodology must be capable of distinguishing rates of change, and breaks in rates of change. We have yet to perfect techniques of doing this for many of the factors involved. For some topics we already claim to distinguish phases: such as are implied in our agricultural, scientific and commercial revolutions, the population explosion and so on. Yet curiously the timing of these phenomena and comparative growth rates are often not clearly established. Even more curiously, there seems to be a marked reluctance to make a serious study of timing.

Timing is frequently regarded as a side issue, perhaps on the assumption that it does not matter precisely when things happened as long as we know why they happened. This has often produced woolly and unsatisfactory history. The agricultural revolution is both theme and title of a recent book by eminent historians[29] but justification of the dating is almost completely absent. Equally striking is the way in which modern and reputable historians have found five or six technical revolutions in British agriculture between the thirteenth and nineteenth centuries (see Chapter 3). It is beyond the normal reader's capacities to judge the relative significance of these 'revolutions'. The point is not that the historians have been wrong, it is simply that we have not developed adequate standards of comparison. Nevertheless, without trying to minimize the difficulties I would argue that it is both acceptable in principle and possible in practice to distinguish phases of change.

PHASES IN AN INDUSTRIALIZATION PROCESS

The main phases of the purely economic changes must be central ingredients of a time-chart of development. But it is difficult to identify such phases—witness the debates about the meaning of the term 'industrial revolution' and about W. W. Rostow's stage theory. We will return to the term 'industrial revolution' in the next chapter; some features of Rostow's theory will be discussed now. Despite all that has been said against Rostow, his ideas are interesting and stimulating. In common with many others, I owe much to him although disagreeing with most of his basic propositions. The debate about his propositions is now massive and in some state of confusion, partly because Rostow has consistently tried to give his retreats the appearance of advances. This adds an element of incoherence to an already difficult debate. For instance, part of his latest definition of the 'take-off' is almost identical with part of his earlier definition of the 'maturity' stage—and in the earlier work he wrote that maturity began some forty years after the take-off had ended.[30]

[29] J. D. Chambers and G. E. Mingay, 1966.
[30] W. W. Rostow, 1963a, p. 8. Cf. Rostow, 1960, p. 10.

Sadly perhaps, that colourful phrase 'the take-off' has outlived its usefulness, for a number of important reasons. Rostow is now distinguishing between a 'take-off' and an 'abortive industrial surge', and admits that it is only possible to distinguish them retrospectively because a true take-off can only be identified *after* the economy has demonstrated the capacity to shift from one set of leading sectors to another.[31] It is perhaps typical of Rostow that he does not attempt to reconcile this idea and its implications with other characteristics of his take-off. Indeed, I believe that they are irreconcilable.

Rostow's fundamental difficulty is that the initiation of modern growth does not always lead to industrialization. This is why he is now forced to talk about an abortive industrial surge. However, he skirts an important issue because he does not tell us whether the difference between take-off and abortive surge can be traced to inadequate pre-conditioning or to the character of early modern growth, or both. I would argue strongly that *either* can cause an upsurge of growth to fall away. Growth is not likely to proceed far if the agricultural sector is almost entirely subsistence when growth begins, and equally growth is likely to falter if the agricultural sector fails to continue to adjust at an appropriate speed as modern growth continues. Rostow is perhaps recognizing this (or the difficulties which it creates) when he admits that it is only possible to identify take-off after it has occurred. The real difficulty for him is to reconcile this with his old 'central proposition' about the take-off which he reaffirmed in 1963.[32] Here we are directed to the idea of an initial thrust to the economy, launched on an adequately prepared base, powered by an engine of economic transformation (leading sector) which is powerful enough to suck other parts of the economy into the upward thrust. There is a definite inference of inevitability once the initial thrust is delivered, and surely this is quite compatible with the idea that a true take-off occurs only if and when the economy can develop a new leading sector—as the thrust of the first leading sector subsides.

Rostow's difficulty is truly profound. On the one hand he is protesting that the forces set up by the take-off are only potential forces which continue to require 'active exploitation' if the process is to continue. Only when the society has *demonstrated* the capacity to develop new leading sectors can take-off be identified or even be said to have occurred. On the other hand he argues that a true take-off is a 'definitive transition', and such is its impact on society that we are unlikely to see a true lapsing back. Poetically he compares it to the loss of innocence, but

---

[31] W. W. Rostow, 1963a, p. 8.
[32] *Ibid.*, p. xvii.

apparently the maiden can later awaken to discover that she has been a virgin all the time.

Much of the confusion in the debate probably arises from Rostow's tenacity in clinging to the idea of a pre-conditioning period leading to take-off. Surely it would be wiser to think in terms of the conditioning of various elements leading to a fully integrated industrial society, and not to the take-off—i.e. not to the beginning but to the end of the industrial revolution, when the transformation to a mature industrial society has been consummated. We could broadly define a mature or integrated industrial society as one where all economic factors have been drawn in to the exchange economy and where institutions and social and intellectual values are compatible with continuing growth and indeed are determined by an expectation of continuing growth. The conditioning which leads to this society will take place both before and during the initial phases of modern growth. Substantial growth can occur before the whole community is reconciled to a growth outlook. We can also recognize that *some* conditioning is necessary before modern growth begins, but Rostow's over-emphasis of the latter point is made, in the end, at the expense of clarity and essential flexibility.

The advantages of this view of conditioning are many. First, it removes one of the problems which worries Simon Kuznets when he doubts whether any meaningful distinction can be drawn between the pre-conditioning and take-off, because some factors are said to change in both stages.[33] It is perfectly logical to retain a distinction if we regard conditioning as leading to integrated growth—conditioning may take place prior to *and* concurrent with initial modern growth. For instance, some conditioning of agriculture may be essential before modern growth is initiated, but it is unrealistic to suppose that the whole of agriculture will be transformed at this stage; during transition it will continue to adjust to the newly growing economy, until virtually the whole agricultural community is drawn into the modern exchange economy. It is only if and when this happens that the economy can be regarded as that of an integrated industrial society. If agriculture does not adjust to the growth of the modern sector it may retard or completely choke progress. This means both that modern growth can be initiated before conditioning is completed and that failure of suitable conditioning during modern growth may cause it to disappear. That, of course, is why 'take-off' is a misleading term, because success does not come only from an initial thrust: it depends equally on a continuing process of adjustment.

Further, Rostow's idea of a definite pattern of pre-conditioning prior to take-off is too rigid. Some countries have progressed more quickly

[33] S. Kuznets, 1963, pp. 36 ff.

than others through initial growth to integrated growth. Therefore it is only reasonable to suppose that pre-conditioning will always be the same when modern growth is initiated if we assume that the full conditioning of all elements is equally compressible in time. It seems highly unlikely that all are equally compressible, and if they are not, we cannot assume, for example, that agriculture will always have reached the same stage of conditioning when modern growth is initiated. Compare, for instance, Japanese agriculture with British agriculture at Rostow's take-off dates.

In the late nineteenth century Japanese agriculture was dominated by its closely integrated village society. It was 'a vast and populous hinterland of conservatism'.[34] True, agriculture responded for a time to growth in the economy, but this was achieved mainly by the spread of techniques already practised by the best farmers.[35] Once this diffusion of techniques had run its course, the innovative limitations of village-bound farmers were reflected in agricultural stagnation.[36] The village remained powerful in Japan partly because there were few men of the kind who led innovation in England—gentlemen farmers and large leaseholders.

Comparative studies assume that industrialization will have common features, either because all industrial societies acquire common characteristics at some point or points in their histories, or because there will be a common pattern of development during the transition, or perhaps both. Rostow's construction implies both, and this is a fundamental error. It seems to be a mistake to fit investigations into a common mould at the outset, because there will almost certainly be variation. There are obvious variations in the speed of development and I would be surprised if this did not also mean variations in the dynamic relationships within development.

Since what we are seeking to do is to generalize or systematize, we must assume *some* common features or our investigations will be purposeless. However, Rostow's framework of investigation (assuming a common pattern of development) is in effect assuming a common pattern of interrelationships: the process can be stretched or squeezed but this will not affect the interrelationships involved. I believe that this will be proved wrong but, more important, I believe that to use it as a starting-point or framework of investigation will inhibit those investigations, because such an approach suggests that it is irrelevant to investigate the pattern of interrelationships in the history of a particular industrialization except as an illustration or elaboration of the general case.

[34] Thomas C. Smith, 1959, p. 210.
[35] Y. Hayami and S. Yamada, 1968.
[36] K. Ohkawa and H. Rosovsky, 1960.

That countries do not have a common pattern of development is certainly implied in our second qualification to Hirschman's idea, the qualification which emphasizes the effect of independent events upon the progress of the economy and the society.

THE TIME-CHART OF DEVELOPMENT

What I propose is not a common model, it is simply a common form of investigation: a procedure. Ideally the first stage should be to delineate the main economic aggregates and rates of growth. However, lack of data may force us to be content with a series of snapshots rather than a moving picture. The story may have to be built around points of reference, and a particularly important point will be the beginning of integrated modern growth. The other reference marks such as the initiation of modern growth may be fitted into the chart, but there will be no assumption of any constant or unique relationships between the elements at such points. They will be interesting stopping places in the economic journey, but we will not expect the same stops nor the same conditions to be found at these stopping places for everyone who sets out for the same destination.

The second task will be to decide which social and economic values and institutions to build into the chart—which of them were potential restraints upon economic growth in the period of study. (We probably know more about this question than any other.) Next we must try to fit these factors into the chart by distinguishing their main phases of change. Fourth, we must try to analyse the characteristics or the maturity of each factor at the beginning of its relevant phase of change, and we must investigate the independent influences on the timing of change for each of the potential restraints. Fifth, we must try to see whether any of these factors actually acted as restraints at various times or whether they responded smoothly to the pressures for change in the time context involved. Alternatively, we might try to assess at what time in its history the potential for serious economic restraint disappeared.

The rationale behind the emphasis on chronology is not that it will allow us to identify the key variables by showing which led the way. This is an inadequate criterion, as we have already seen. What it will do is to establish a *pattern* of social and economic adjustments: to show comparatively how the timing of social adjustments related to the timing of changes in the economy. We may hope that this will point the way to causative links, particularly if we can produce a number of studies of industrializations, but in itself it will not establish causal connections.

CONCLUSION

I should like to note specifically that I am not proposing a 'general equilibrium analysis'. Since I regard specialization (partial analysis) as quite indispensable, I am not pleading for its abandonment. Rather I would say that the problem is to delineate more carefully the directions and purposes of partial studies. If the questions we currently ask cannot, or do not, illuminate the broad theme of the subject we must obviously seek other questions. Of course it is not easy to decide whether a particular approach will illuminate the theme, but at least it is clear that the old questions have not provided satisfactory answers. It is simply not good enough to pretend that they have done so.

Perhaps the most serious deficiency of the old questions is that they imply an oversimplified concept of the growth mechanism. It is not a mousetrap game in which obstacles are rolled over one by one. This kind of thinking seems to be behind the 'most important cause' and the 'initial stimulus' approaches. Economic growth is in fact a process of subtle and continuous interaction between a number of factors. The social environment determines the limits within which economic man can work, but as he works he gradually alters the society and so expands the limits. It is the subtle interplays resulting which give the process its complexity and its fascination. Whether my particular method will achieve useful results will depend firstly on whether the information it produces will have any instructional value, and secondly on whether it is workable. The methodological problems involved are much more complex than my sketch implies, and the final test must come at research level. This means that the issues raised in this chapter will not be settled by a conclusive debate. It also follows that all students of the British industrial revolution must be involved, not just a few methodologists. I am convinced that our present methodology is seriously deficient and purposeless in a broad sense. It will require continuous thought and vigilance to see that a broad sense of purpose is maintained by scholars researching particular topics. We must, of course, understand how we hope to do this and what we hope to achieve. At the moment I do not believe that we do.

In this chapter I have argued that two weaknesses are common to economist and historian: first, that social influences on industrialization are neglected in a functional sense, and second, that interactions—and particularly mutual interactions—are effectively ignored. The neglect of mutual interactions may be partly because their importance is unrecognized; but perhaps it is simply that we realize that mutual interaction analysis is impossibly complex. Economic historians may sidestep this complexity by developing a time-chart approach, as a useful substitute for mutual interaction analysis; but a time-chart approach demands a much more rigorous approach to chronology than is currently in vogue.

FURTHER READING

AYAL, E. B.: 'Value Systems and Economic Development in Japan and Thailand'.

EASTERLIN, R. A.: 'Is There a Need for Historical Research on Under-development?'

FLINN, M. W.: *The Origins of the Industrial Revolution.*
'Social Theory and the Industrial Revolution.'

GOULD, J. D.: 'Hypothetical History'.

HABAKKUK, H. J.: 'Historical Experience of Economic Development'.

HAGEN, E.: 'A Framework for Analysing Economic and Political Change'.
'How Economic Growth Begins: A Theory of Social Change'.

HARTWELL, R. M.: 'The Causes of the Industrial Revolution. An Essay in Methodology'.
The Causes of the Industrial Revolution in England. (Editor's introduction)
The Industrial Revolution and Economic Growth (Chs. 7 and 8).

HIRSCHMAN, A. O.: *The Strategy of Economic Development.*

HOSELITZ, B. F.: 'Non-economic Barriers to Economic Development'.

LEIBENSTEIN, H.: 'Allocative Efficiency versus X Efficiency'.

LEWIS, W. A.: *The Theory of Economic Growth.*

MCCLELLAND, D. C. and WINTER, D. G.: *Motivating Economic Growth.*

MARTIN, KURT and KNAPP, JOHN: *The Teaching of Development Economics.*

MOORE, W. E.: *Industrialization and Labour: Social Aspects of Economic Development.*

ROSTOW, W. W. (ed.): *The Economics of Take-off into Sustained Growth.* (Introduction, Chs. 1, 2)

SMELSER, N.: *The Sociology of Economic Life.*

SUPPLE, B. A.: 'Economic History and Economic Underdevelopment'.

2 Perspectives

DEFINING 'THE INDUSTRIAL REVOLUTION'

In the previous chapter we explored the methodological problems of studying industrialization. The term 'industrial revolution' (which we can equate with the transition to industrialization) has been subject to such attack by historians that it may be useful to examine it. Apart from the desire for linguistic precision, we require a precise working definition if we wish to build a time-chart around a transition phase. The second half of this chapter will consist of a hypothetical scheme of the British experience leading to industrialization, to give some perspective to the discussion of the individual topics.

Many criteria suggested as the distinguishing features of the industrial revolution have been found to be unsatisfactory because they are not unique to any particular period.[1] Factory organization, the use of power in manufacturing, specialization of labour, are all to be found in Britain and other countries before the industrial revolution. Furthermore, factories and the use of power in manufacturing were not pervasive until well after the industrial revolution is thought to have begun. This means that arbitrary assumptions are almost inevitable in applying these criteria. Consequently they are easily attacked. Further, some criteria are inadequate because they can be used to show that the country has experienced other industrial revolutions: historians can find an industrial revolution under almost every stone.[2] If the term is to be useful it must apply to a unique phase of the economic growth of a particular country.

Objections to the term have sometimes had a semantic flavour, though points of substance are involved. One such objection is based on a false analogy with a political revolution.[3] It is false because it would be quite impossible for an economic revolution to be an overnight change, as a political coup may be. In the economic sphere we are simply using a different time perspective. In economic terms the period of the classical industrial revolution was a time when economic advance

[1] G. N. Clark, 1953.
[2] *Ibid.*, pp. 12 f.; and D. C. Coleman, 1956.
[3] G. N. Clark, 1953, pp. 7 ff.

produced a much more fundamental change in man's economic life than any other period of similar span, and in that sense it is a revolution —an economic revolution.

More substantially, this line of attack claims that the time-span of the whole process is so long that, if the antecedent conditions and the consequences are included, the word 'revolution' is obviously meaningless.[4] There were, indeed, antecedent conditions which were essential to the industrial revolution, and some of these developed over generations or centuries. We can trace the beginning of the process back to the Renaissance at least. At the other end of the scale the process is continuing, so it is thought, to the present day—we are still under the influence of this economic transition. How then is it possible to speak of a 'revolution', even in economic terms, which has spread over perhaps five hundred years? If one is to follow this argument to its conclusion, however, one is obliged to admit that there have been no revolutions, not even political revolutions. Surely the French Revolution had antecedent conditions and still affects the political lives of Frenchmen. The fallacy in this line of thought is the implicit assumption that it is impossible to distinguish between antecedents and the 'revolution': they are apparently seen as parts of one and the same process. However, for us to assume that the 'revolution' has no separate existence, it is necessary to show that it inevitably followed the antecedent conditions. Perhaps it is true that there comes a point where conditions are such that revolution (or the beginnings of it) cannot be averted, but this is probably only shortly before the revolution begins. We can say both that the French Revolution was the outcome of conditions which go back into the early eighteenth century or earlier, and that it could have been averted by different policies a comparatively short time before it happened. This applies equally to the British industrial revolution. Obviously the antecedent conditions and the revolution were not bound together as part of an indissoluble process. This is not to say that the antecedent conditions were not significant in subsequent events, only that the two are historically and conceptually distinguishable. This implies that it is quite legitimate to distinguish the revolutionary phase, and to give it a name.

At the other end of the scale it is true that the economy is still changing but this need not invalidate the concept of an 'industrial revolution', because the essence of an industrial society is that it undergoes more or less continuous change. It is certainly true, however, that the problem of identification is more acute for an industrial than for a political revolution. Even those who agree that the term is legitimate have been unable to agree on a working definition of 'the industrial revolution'.

[4] *Ibid.*, pp. 28 ff.

The only satisfactory definition is one involving not only the purely economic changes but also their social consequences.[5] The industrial revolution was not just a transformation of industry or even of the economy: it was also a fundamental change in the kind of society. It involved realignment of economic life, from an agrocentric to an urban-industrial economy, and it was also inextricably bound up with social, political and intellectual changes of a most far-reaching kind. The industrial revolution is thus distinguished by its effect upon the very basis of society. This, for example, is the difference between the classic industrial revolution, and Nef's industrial revolution between 1540 and 1640, which left society[6] fundamentally unchanged.

The classic industrial revolution brought a number of fundamental changes in British society. The external appearance of society altered— the majority of people were urban dwellers, their occupations as well as their dwellings divorced from the land; the ambitions of society altered —at the upper levels land ownership lost its social position and the measure of social achievement was more material and wide-ranging. Political power had been wrested from the landed classes, though the process was prolonged by the cunning with which it was yielded by degrees. Perhaps one of the most nebulous but far-reaching developments was in society's outlook towards change. A basically static society has institutions and attitudes which favour continued stability— attitudes where change is accepted unwillingly and only by the strongest persuasion or coercion. The industrial society on the other hand, is both inured to change and expectant that it will continue. It may take measures to ameliorate the difficulties created by over-rapid change, but fundamentally it tolerates and expects continuous change. The full significance of this difference is perhaps not sufficiently appreciated.

A definition of the industrial revolution therefore must embrace a wide range of social and other factors—the justification for labelling it an *industrial* revolution is that these changes were wrought by the speed and depth of industrial or economic growth. However, although the revolution is brought about by speed of economic growth, it is impossible for a number of reasons to sustain a definition based only on the speed of growth:

(a) Rates of growth in themselves can be misleading because it is easy to get high rates of growth in the initial stages when industry (or whatever is being measured) is small. Although its rate of growth may be high its size makes it insignificant.

(b) Rates of growth of industry depend upon the growth of the economy and conditions of growth generally; for example, the rate of

[5] D. C. Coleman, 1956.
[6] J. U. Nef, 1932, Vol. I, p. 165; and Nef, 1934.

growth of manufacturing in Australia was higher between 1860 and 1890 than in any stage of British industrial growth until perhaps the mid-nineteenth century, yet no one would describe this as an industrial revolution in Australia. The high growth rates are explained partly by the small size of manufacturing in the beginning but also by the very high rates of economic growth generally—with vigorous migration, land settlement and urban construction.[7] Moreover, the very fact that another country is already industrialized alters the conditions in which subsequent industrial revolutions occur. Techniques, management, training facilities, institutions, etc., may be partly copied or borrowed from the industrialized country—perhaps influencing the rate of growth of the late starter. There may also be negative factors, in the competition from the established industries of the country already industrialized.

(c) The rate of growth of industry may be actually higher (or no lower) after the industrial revolution. If the industrial revolution is a transition, this implies that part of the economy is not modernized until the end of the revolution. Hence the whole of the economy will be modernized only when the industrial revolution is complete; and consequently technical advance may have a more immediate and widespread influence. Rates of change may therefore be higher in a fully industrialized community than in one partly industrialized.

(d) A distinction on the basis of rates of change must be entirely arbitrary. Why should a growth rate of 3·7 per cent per annum be taken as an indication of an industrial revolution, and not one of 3·2 per cent per annum? It is virtually impossible to substantiate any boundary you may select: the selection itself will have to be based upon other criteria—perhaps a preconceived notion about when the industrial revolution began.

It is essential to develop a definition which emphasizes the transition from one kind of society to another, since this was the unique aspect of the industrial revolution. There are immense practical problems, however. The first is the difficulty of developing objective measures of some of the key variables; and even if we could do so the problem of weighting might be impossible, with many heterogeneous factors involved. A second set of difficulties arises because none of the social factors we have mentioned is likely to be entirely stationary before the transitional period. For instance, men of progressive ideas exist in any community, and the number of such men was almost certainly growing before the industrial revolution began. Indeed, it will be part of my argument that there was increasing flexibility in the social system before the main transition began, and that this was absolutely essential to the

[7] N. G. Butlin, *Investment in Australian Economic Development 1861–1900* (Cambridge University Press, London, 1964).

transition itself. Social flexibility on the necessary scale could not suddenly have begun without some prelude.

Now this means that even if we could reduce the various social aspects to some common denominator, there would still remain the vital problem of how to make use of the data. In fact, using an index of social change may involve arbitrary dividing lines in the same way that we found using growth rates of industry involved using arbitrary dividing lines. Clearly it is necessary to identify a long-run deviation in the speed of social change, and with all the difficulties in mind it seems unlikely that a satisfactory direct measure can be devised for the purpose.

It may be reasonable to identify the phase broadly. The balance of society had obviously tipped by the second half of the nineteenth century: it was a very different society from that of, say, 1700. However, the problem of identifying the exact timing of the critical phase of transition remains. If we accept that the balance did swing—that a society with a basically new philosophy had been produced—and if we accept also that this had been produced by economic change, we may link the two ideas to produce a working definition. In practical terms it comes close to definitions often used now. What we seek to identify is the period of economic growth which *ex post* we know was associated with a fundamental change in society.

Thus 'the industrial revolution' is defined as a period of rapid economic growth sufficient to induce a fundamental change in the structure of the economy, and the nature of society. Applying the definition involves first a broad identification of when society underwent a fundamental change in its character and outlook—an identification made largely on subjective grounds but which would nevertheless probably find general approval from historians. Second, we need to identify the beginnings of the rapid economic growth associated in time with the transformation of society. This may be established on conventional grounds of a discernible upturn in production and productivity per capita.

On this basis I would agree with the consensus of current opinion that the British industrial revolution began in the 1780s. In justification I would say that some kind of fundamental transition occurred in Britain in the eighteenth and nineteenth centuries; by the second half of the nineteenth century, British society was obviously fundamentally different from what it was in 1700. If it is agreed that this difference was caused by economic change, and more specifically industrial growth, then it is clear that the industrial revolution (the transition) occurred sometime between 1700 and 1900. Even those who disagree most violently with the term 'industrial revolution' agree that some fundamental change occurred in British society in the eighteenth and nineteenth centuries, and that this was induced by economic factors.

In the second phase of the argument, we must identify the beginning of the industrial growth which had repercussions upon society. The identification is based upon production and productivity changes, using partly Hoffmann's [8] but more particularly Deane and Cole's estimates. [9] The conclusion is that the industrial upsurge began in the 1780s. Perhaps this will surprise the reader who recalls the emphasis which Deane and Cole give to economic growth from 1740 or 1745 on. However, there are two aspects of this earlier period of growth which appear to mark it off from the later period. Although by Deane and Cole's reckoning the period began with an upward movement in per capita productivity, when the whole forty-year period is considered, per capita output only grew at the same rate as in the first forty years of the century. [10] Thus, although this was a period of comparative boom (because population was growing more rapidly perhaps) it was not a period of fundamental change in the economy. Further, it appears that those industries which expanded during the boom were mainly traditional industries—the woollen industry, tin, copper and coal—which still used traditional methods. [11] None of the industries which were later to be at the forefront of productivity changes seem to have played a major part in this boom. Consequently it is no surprise that there was little increase in productivity in this period. After 1780, on the other hand, we find new industries coming into greater prominence, which seems to be reflected in a definite upturn in per capita productivity. Here seems to lie the beginning of the economic surge which led to a restructured society.

Nevertheless, even if the early boom was not part of the crucial transitional phase, there are good reasons for believing that it was an essential prelude to that phase. For instance, it was probably essential to new kinds of investment decisions that an attitude of optimism should prevail early in the industrial revolution. Such optimism is not produced overnight—and this may be reason enough for supposing that the boom of 1740–80 was an essential aspect of the process of British industrialization. This should serve to remind us that the term 'industrial revolution' only identifies the crucial transitional phase, which was fundamental but was nevertheless a *phase*; the whole story does not begin nor end there.

If the industrial revolution began in the 1780s, when did it end? If an essential aspect of the transition was a restructuring of the economy,

[8] W. G. Hoffmann, 1955.
[9] Phyllis Deane and W. A. Cole, 1962, particularly Ch. 2.
[10] *Ibid.*, p. 80.   [11] *Ibid.*, pp. 52–9.

perhaps we can identify the end by locating the end of this readjustment. One difficulty is that restructuring of the economy continues even after the economy has obviously become industrialized. Even mature industrial economies continually change, with the growing importance of the tertiary sector. Perhaps only a rough estimate is possible, in terms of the swing in the balance between primary and secondary industry; although changes in this relationship may continue afterwards, the most important phase may be discernible. In Britain the position was complicated by her heavy reliance upon foreign trade, and her policy of allowing unrestrained foreign competition in primary products, which together brought continued decline of her agriculture—probably well beyond what could have been expected. British agriculture plunged down and down in comparative importance throughout the nineteenth century and well into the twentieth century. Nevertheless, it does appear that the marked swing to manufactures, obvious before 1850, became less pronounced after the middle of the century. By then the main features of the transition in the British economy had been achieved and Britain had become predominantly an industrial society, though she later became even more dependent upon manufacturing.

A SKETCH OF BRITISH ECONOMIC CHANGE

I have proposed that research should work towards producing a time-chart or critical-path format. The kind of hypothetical framework involved will be illustrated by a schema of British economic development, leading up to and into the industrial revolution.

It will be obvious that the schema in itself has no special qualities and is similar to many such outlines of British economic development. However, its purpose is profoundly different: it is not intended as a set of conclusions but only as a set of broad hypotheses. It is the start, not the culmination of our work. The next and most important step is to derive research topics from it. One function of the general outline is to remind us of the many social and economic factors at work in the period so that we shall be constantly aware of potential influences. Also, and most important, it is intended as a reminder of the purposes of industrialization histories—to produce a rounded explanation.

In the first half of the sixteenth century Britain began to emerge from economic lassitude. This emergence had unique features: it was much more commercial and international than any previous period of expansion. The main aspects of this growth were the growth of London as a commercial and industrial metropolis, the expansion of the ancient woollen industry, particularly as an export industry, and an accompanying though regionalized reaction in agriculture. The expansion of the economy was not peculiar to Britain, which is not surprising since a major part of the British expansion was connected with external markets. Nevertheless Britain was amongst the leaders of this expansion, along with Holland and, for a time, the Italian city states. The nature of this growth suggests that it is connected with geographic discoveries and a consequent expansion of trade. This conclusion need not be based only on Earl Hamilton's thesis of the effects of inflation (the Price Revolution) on profits and hence on business enterprise.[12] As long as gold and silver were universally acceptable for international payment, the influx into Spain provided purchasing power which stimulated trade in commodities throughout Europe. Thus the purchasing power of Spanish bullion provided a market for goods; and the growth of the Spanish market had multiplying effects—both directly in those countries selling to Spain and indirectly in those countries who increased sales to Spain's trading partners. The trade stimulated by bullion was carried further by spices and later tobacco, sugar and rice. In Britain the expansion of trade profoundly influenced a substantial minority of the population. By 1700 the population of London had risen to half a million, or nearly 9 per cent of the population of England and Wales;[13] and a substantial proportion of the population had become dependent on the wool trade, particularly in the West Country and Norfolk and increasingly in the West Riding. The growth of London and the woollen industry had reacted upon agriculture, particularly where ley-farming offered scope for expanding output to create a surplus for sale. However, commercial food production was less influenced by the expansion of the textile industry than it might have been because of the semi-rural character of much of the industry, which meant that workers drew part of their food requirements from their own small plots. There must have been some influence, but not enough to force a throughgoing local agricultural commercialization. It did, however, bring to parts of rural Britain some knowledge of commercial exchange for money—perhaps less important for its influence on agricultural technique than for the increasing acquaintance it gave with the abstractions of money. It is true that large parts of the rural economy were almost untouched by commercialism, but by the end of the seventeenth century a substantial minority had come to accept commercial exchange and a money economy as the determinants of their economic lives. Others had some experience of money as a medium of exchange and the market as a means of disposing of surplus produce,

[12] E. J. Hamilton, 1929.
[13] Phyllis Deane and W. A. Cole, 1962, p. 7.

but this was peripheral to their lives; it provided the cream, but not the bread, of their existence. Such people would have been distressed but not shattered by the regression of the commercial market.

The changing economy must have influenced men's attitudes to cities. The continuous growth of London reflected a new attitude towards urban life by more and more people. In addition, some of the technical problems of the exchange economy were being recognized and at least partly solved in this period. Internally the exchange of goods became more sophisticated, and there were improvements in transferring money from one part of the country to another. Similar progress can be seen in international trade; here the Dutch were for long the masters. The shipping industry matured: 'share' investment in ships developed, necessitated by larger ships and longer voyages which meant that few individuals could undertake the investment alone. The British became highly skilled in shipping organization because of their concentration on long-distance trade.

The first influence of the growth of European commerce was therefore the creation of a substantial minority who were completely dependent upon commercial exchange for their livelijood, and who developed appropriate institutions for this commercial life. A further substantial group became more aware of commercial practices, accepting them as partly relevant to their lives.

It is difficult to say what proportion of the population fell into these two groups by the seventeenth century, though we may say confidently that Britain was no longer feudal by this time. In some areas the division of labour was quite marked, but we have no means of knowing how widespread this had become, nor of judging the sophistication of the industrial village economy. It is possible that some part of the division of labour was on a purely village scale, little removed, if at all, from a barter economy. No doubt a proportion of people used money reluctantly and fearfully, and conducted nearly all their transactions within their own village, but how many? Unfortunately the problem is to trace *stages* in a gradual evolution of commercialism.

It is probably true that the majority of men were largely untouched by the new aspects of European life. Nevertheless, the consequences were profound and far-reaching because those most affected were in the upper classes of society. Consequently the intellectual and ethical life of the community was deeply influenced. The changing circumstance of the upper crust of society caused a fundamental rethinking of the tenets of that society. This rethinking was not specifically British but European, though its precise form varied from country to country. The influence of the stirring of men's ideas can be seen in religion, science, politics, and even the class system.

It is probably true that these intellectual stirrings were closely connected with the economic awakening of Europe, following the geographic discoveries. However, it is not necessary to argue, after the fashion of Marx, that economic change was inevitable and that this in turn determined the whole nature of society. At the same time it would be foolish to suppose that economic progress did not challenge values, institutions, and attitudes which were based on a stagnant economy; and it would be equally foolish to suppose that economic progress can proceed very far in the face of immovable values unsuited to progress. Here we return to our earlier emphasis upon mutual inter-action between the economy, institutions and social values.

In the early modern period a profound and pervasive religious struggle edged its way through Europe. Some have seen a direct connection between this struggle and economic progress in this era. It was certainly not simply a theological dispute: it was part of a fundamental confrontation within society of the old ethos and the new. It may be unwise to put religion so exclusively in the middle of the stage as some writers do. True, religion was connected more with the ethos of society than it is today and this is the justification for studying the problem from this angle. Nevertheless there were various aspects of this ethos which came under attack, and some people who were prepared to change one aspect were not prepared to change others. Luther, for instance, was opposed to the new science. The struggle between the ethos of a stagnant and unworldly society and the realities of the new economic situation raised different problems at different times to men in Italy, Switzerland, the Netherlands, Britain and Southern Germany.

The struggle was complicated and confused by man's tendency to think of morals and ethics as immutable. Add to this the possibility that men might see the problem differently according to where they lived, whether in the light of the happy picture of Defoe's West Riding, or the shadow of the degradation of the Durham coalminers. No wonder, then, that the conflict raged so long, that some saw it more clearly than others, and that individuals often seem confused and self-contradictory in their ideas. Nor should we think of the conflict as an inevitable triumph for the new. As in Spain, the challenge to established values might be defeated. Even where new forces gained ascendancy, a continual struggle might be necessary against an effective relapse—the gelling of a new form of rigid moral orthodoxy. For these reasons the story is not always as easy to follow as the labels 'Catholic' and 'Protestant' imply. Sometimes the so-called Protestant might be committed to rigid ethics suited to a stagnant society. On the other hand there were changes within the Catholic Church as we can see in the work of the

Jesuits. Indeed, as Bronowski and Mazlish point out, the difference between heretics and radicals was sometimes only a hair's breadth.[14]

Some see religious change as a positive stimulant to new economic practice (see Chapter 8). It is more likely that religious change served gradually to remove old moral restraints upon economic activity. The process was not simple, however. It is not possible to say unequivocally that religion came to welcome the newly wealthy merchant, nor even to say that it clearly came to tolerate him or his methods. It may be more correct to say that religious attitudes to wealth and to certain business practices became more ambiguous. With growing emphasis on the rule of conscience, the old clear-cut condemnation of 'progressive' business methods disappeared. It was, however, a long process. Echoes of the old morality were to be heard in the eighteenth century even from the most progressive of the divines. But if they were not entirely convinced and convincing, their utterances were diverse and ambiguous enough to give licence to all but the obviously rapacious. Moreover, part of the process was simply that religion lost its pervasive hold over men's lives. This transition from the other-worldliness of medieval life was enormously important to subsequent industrialization. It is true that some men are always prepared to defy the restraints imposed by social values—the moneylender and the land-shark can be found everywhere; but there are natural limits to the number of men who will defy society's *mores*. For an economy to become and remain dynamic, social values must be suitable for, or at least impose no serious limits on, a large number of enterprising businessmen and their practices.

Political life was also altering under the pressure of new economic forces. Minority groups had won freedom from rampant economic exploitation for the benefit of the old aristocracy. In England it had become politically impossible to impose arbitrary and crushing taxation upon new economic classes as a means of preventing a challenge to the economic supremacy of the old order. This was a freedom which had yet to be established in many European countries, and which even today is still not established in parts of Asia, Africa and South America.

A measure of political stability had also been achieved by the eighteenth century, though by twentieth-century standards the eighteenth century was still unstable. It is however very difficult to measure political stability and its effects.

The intellectual life of Europe was transformed also in this period by the scientific revolution and the Enlightenment (see Chapter 5). The scientific revolution was pragmatically based and it was also dependent upon a new intellectual structure. The methods of analysis

[14] J. Bronowski and Bruce Mazlish, 1960, p. 77.

which were the essence of the scientific revolution gave man a new ability to solve practical problems. These methods were at first applied to a limited range of great problems and were entirely the province of an intellectual elite and their patrons, but by the middle of the eighteenth century many in the middle ranks of society realized how useful science could be in solving the production problems of an expanding economy. They learnt what science had to offer and their technical abilities correspondingly improved. The intellectual penetration of new modes of thought went further and further down the social scale, and in the nineteenth century pervaded and underlay the education which was gradually organized for the lower classes. Its effect was not, of course, identical to the effect upon upper and middle ranks, but it was nevertheless influential in producing a community whose habits of thought differed from those of people in traditional societies. The penetration of the lower ranks had the twin advantages of preparing their minds to work with more sophisticated machinery and increasing the range of people from which the community could draw its engineers, designers and scientists. Thus by degrees the community had transformed its intellectual traditions and habitual modes of thought to fit the requirements of the changing economy.

In Britain the evolutionary changes, both economic and intellectual, were as profound as anywhere in Europe. No doubt this was partly because of her geographic position, and partly by chance—as with her political liberalism. From the end of the seventeenth century a period of economic change was superimposed upon Britain's gradually evolving social flexibility, which accelerated the process and finally brought new economic forms in the industrial revolution.

The economic changes immediately preceding the industrial revolution had two phases. The first, lasting until about 1740, was a period of mild prosperity. It was the outcome of a series of good harvests, the extension of cultivation into lighter soils, and the expansion of export markets based upon the newer cheaper woollens and worsteds made in northern England. The economic benefits accrued mainly to middle and lower groups who thus enjoyed high living standards for that age. This was the golden age of the English labourer. The boom in exports slackened after 1720 but good harvests and low population growth maintained living standards. For most men life was easy though not exciting.

Boom conditions were experienced after the War of Austrian Succession. Exports grew rapidly. Although seasons were not so favourable, the spread of improved farming methods maintained the supply of food, despite a noticeably higher rate of population growth. Markets were expanding as working-class numbers increased, and the workers managed to retain the higher living standards to which they had grown accustomed early in the eighteenth century.

True, this burst of economic activity did not bring any profound changes in production techniques, nor did any new industries attain enough importance to affect productivity. The boom was based upon some improvement in agriculture, but this was not yet enough to outpace the growth of population. Manufacturing expanded but it was an expansion of traditional industries using traditional methods—it was the woollen, copper, tin and coal industries which account for most expansion. Thus the economy ballooned out but did not alter its shape— there was no great improvement in productivity on the whole: the industrial revolution had not yet begun.

Nevertheless the existence of the boom between 1740 and 1780 had important consequences. Indeed, it is doubtful if the industrial revolution could have begun in the 1780s without it, since it produced an environment of optimism and expansion. There were a number of important aspects of this environment.

First, it encouraged an atmosphere of optimism, from which emerged a class of industrial entrepeneurs willing to organize new forms of production and to commit a growing proportion of their money to fixed capital. Second, it was a condition of the accelerating rate of population growth. The growth of population assured a growing labour supply for the expanding economy. Third, it brought a new awareness that agricultural improvement was vital to an expanding economy, and probably a more widespread readiness to experiment with new agricultural techniques and organization. This paved the way for a remarkable response by agriculture to the prolonged and rapid population growth which followed. This was essential if the gains in the export potential of the economy were not to be dissipated by large imports of foodstuffs. Fourth, it expanded and strengthened trading connections essential to the industrial revolution, since Britain needed imports of raw materials and to a lesser extent foodstuffs, and a complementary market for her products. When, late in the eighteenth century, Britain turned to the U.S.A. for her raw cotton, the latter adjusted very quickly to the new situation. She was probably only able to do so because of her strong existing trade links with Britain, and because she had a long history of commercial agricultural production. These characteristics of the American agrarian scene emerged well before 1780: the foundations laid by tobacco and rice were vital to the growth of the cotton trade.

Transport improvement obviously helped to transform the economy; but it is not clear whether the transport improvement simply followed economic requirements or played a more dynamic role at times. The river improvement schemes and turnpike building early in the eighteenth century may have been a stimulus contributing to the boom conditions after 1740. However, the turnpike probably had little commercial significance apart from speeding up communications. River improvements lowered costs, but their influence was limited to particular industries such as coal mining. Both the canal boom of the late eighteenth century and the rail boom of the mid-nineteenth century probably began as a response to specific requirements for more efficient transport. Both booms however acquired a momentum of their own, which must have brought external economies to the whole business world. But it is difficult to prove that this was so, and it may well be that the bulk of the boom was simply filling in a gap which had been building up for some time. The early constructions perhaps served to demonstrate the full extent of this gap. Certainly the construction boom itself had linkage effects which obviously stimulated the economy, and this may have been vital to particular industries at certain stages; but the exact relationship between transport improvements and the growth of the economy is one of the least understood aspects of the British industrial revolution.

The expansion of demand and its relationship to population growth has been sadly neglected in historical literature (see Chapter 4). The growth of London in the seventeenth century must have meant that more and more of the lower classes were thrown into the commercial world. Early in the eighteenth century there may have been a further shift, as cheap and plentiful foodstuffs allowed more people an excess of income to spend on manufactured goods (though it is difficult to judge the net result, since farmers' incomes may have suffered). As population expanded in the second half of the century, and as a greater proportion of the population were drawn into the market-place, there was probably a more spectacular commercial penetration of the lower class market, though we know very little about the speed of this penetration and its implications. Nor have we sorted out the links between the growth of demand and cost reductions—both through economies of scale and innovations. We may expect an interlinking, with expansion of demand stimulating the search for improved efficiency and new production techniques, and improved methods—by reducing costs and prices—stimulating demand. However, we have little idea of which factors were crucial at particular times—here is the area where econometric techniques may offer the greatest promise. Was industrial growth mainly through the progressive adjustment of industrial output and techniques to the market situation; or are there important phases when independent cost reductions were able to stimulate market expansions; or is it meaningless to draw such distinctions? Similarly, we have yet to work out the short-term motive for innovations—were they efforts principally to supply expanding markets at a constant price, or to counter rising costs of labour or capital?

In Britain the role of financial institutions was probably passive. Until well into the nineteenth century, banks and other financial institutions played an insignificant part in mobilizing capital and an even smaller role in providing capital for manufacturing. Most of the capital for manufacturing was raised by *ad hoc* expedients; little was raised through institutions. The principal sources were ploughed-back profits of manufactures and the widespread use of trade credits. Sometimes the trade credits were deviously used to provide capital for fixed equipment.[15] Personal loans also helped to mobilize capital.

What we know about capital accumulation suggests that it did not vary much as a proportion of G.N.P. until the early nineteenth century. Economic expansion in the eighteenth century apparently did not increase total capital requirements greatly. This was perhaps partly because the early technical improvements were comparatively inexpensive to implement, but also because there was perhaps an element of capital saving—both in the outlay on equipment in relation to output and through the capital-saving effects of improving transport which reduced the quantity of materials and finished products in transit, and hence the money tied up in stocks. This may be one reason why there seems to be no serious shortage of capital in the eighteenth century despite the various rather crude expedients that entrepreneurs were forced to adopt. Perhaps more savings were mobilized by the more stable capital market after the reform of government finance early in the century. Here is a case where model-building may tell us a great deal: how much capital-saving reduction in inventories took place? What were the capital-output ratios of new methods compared with old? What did all this mean in terms of a change in the structure of capital requirement?

If institutions played an insignificant part in mobilizing credit, they did improve the monetary system. Their relatively sophisticated techniques of transferring money, which had developed mainly for international trade in the seventeenth century, were increasingly employed in the domestic economy as it became more regionalized and interdependent. Such a system of transferring money was essential to the growth of a national economy—as it had been to the expansion of the international economy.

We have noted that the weaknesses of the financial system were partly offset by trade credits. That this happened is partly a reflection of the growing sophistication of selling techniques. This increasing

15 S. Pollard, 1964b.

sophistication had other implications for the industrial revolution too: it was essential to an increasingly commercialized production for a domestic market and to the extension of regional specialization. The structure built by merchants and putters-out in the seventeenth century gradually evolved into the kind of market organization necessary for a commercially-centred and specialized economy.

The role of the government in the industrial revolution was essentially passive. Understandably it offered no incentives for economic change, since it had no economic model at which it could aim. On the other hand it was flexible in the face of changing situations, and its legal and taxation system offered a measure of protection to property owners and avoided crippling taxation upon economic *parvenus*. It also protected some industries from foreign competition. The cotton industry enjoyed some 'infant industry' protection from Indian competition which was partly unintentional, since it was chiefly the woollen industry which the government sought to protect.[16]

SUMMARIZING THE MAIN HISTORICAL PROBLEMS

I now wish to turn to a critical examination of work on particular topics in industrial revolution studies. The essays which follow revolve around what I consider to be the three basic weaknesses of previous studies:

(a) their chronological weakness, which often takes the form of the absence of quantitative distinctions between different phases of growth;

(b) the inadequate treatment of interactions between factors— especially as these interactions continue through the process of growth. It is a special weakness of historians that they claim to be able to distinguish prime causes and straight lines of causation. My argument is that over the long periods involved in transition, there were a number of influences upon the pace of economic change which interacted on each other in a complex and more or less continuous manner.

(c) the inadequate cognizance of social and cultural factors which underlay economic change before and during the industrial revolution.

I will not, however, give equal weight to each of these three points of criticism when discussing each topic. The essays are not intended to analyse fully all the factors contributing to the industrial revolution: there is, for instance, no essay on transport or government policy. Moreover, the topics are often discussed within the limited purposes of this study; the discussion of capital and population growth is by no means as complete as a comprehensive textbook would be.

[16] Sir Edward Baines, 1966, pp. 77–80; A. P. Wadsworth and J. De L. Mann, 1931, pp. 116 ff.

FURTHER READING

On the meaning of the term 'industrial revolution':
BEALES, H. L.: 'The Industrial Revolution'.
CLARK, G. N.: *The Idea of the Industrial Revolution.*
COLEMAN, D. C.: 'Industrial Growth and Industrial Revolutions'.
DEANE, PHYLLIS: *The First Industrial Revolution.* (Ch. 1)
FLINN, M. W.: *The Origins of the Industrial Revolution.* (Ch. 1)
HARTWELL, R. M.: *The Causes of the Industrial Revolution in England.*
   (Part III of editor's introduction)
   The Industrial Revolution and Economic Growth. (Ch. 3)
MATHIAS, PETER: *The First Industrial Nation.* (Ch. 1)
NEF, J. U.: 'The Progress of Technology and the Growth of Large-
   scale Industry in Great Britain, 1540–1640'.
'The Industrial Revolution Reconsidered'.

On the Industrial Revolution generally:
ASHTON, T. S.: *An Economic History of England: The Eighteenth Century.*
   Economic Fluctuations in England 1700–1800.
   The Industrial Revolution 1760–1830.
CHAMBERS, J. D.: *The Workshop of the World: British Economic History*
   1820–1880.
CLAPHAM, J. H.: *Economic History of Modern Britain.*
COURT, W. H. B.: *A Concise Economic History of Britain from 1750 to*
   Recent Times.
DEANE, PHYLLIS: *The First Industrial Revolution.*
DEANE, PHYLLIS and COLE, W. A.: *British Economic Growth 1688–1959.*
FLINN, M. W.: *The Origins of the Industrial Revolution.*
HABAKKUK, H, J. and POSTAN, M. (eds.): *The Cambridge Economic History*
   of Europe: Vol. VI, *The Industrial Revolution and After.*
HARTWELL, R. M.: *The Industrial Revolution in England.*
   The Industrial Revolution and Economic Growth. (Ch. 6)
HOBSBAWM, E. J.: *Labouring Men: Studies in the History of Labour.*
   Industry and Empire: an Economic History of Britain Since 1750.
LANDES, D.: *The Unbound Prometheus :Technological Change and Indust-*
   rial Development in Western Europe from 1750 to the Present Day.
MANTOUX, P.: *The Industrial Revolution in the Eighteenth Century.*
MATHIAS, PETER: *The First Industrial Nation.*
MITCHELL, B. R. and DEANE, PHYLLIS: *Abstract of British Historical*
   Statistics.

POLLARD, S. and HOLMES, C.: *Documents of European Economic History:* Vol. I, *The Process of Industrialization 1750–1870.*

ROBINSON, E. A. G.: 'The Changing Structure of the British Economy'.

WILSON, C.: *England's Apprenticeship 1603–1763.*

3 Agriculture and the Industrial Revolution

There have been numerous attempts to assess agriculture's role in the industrial revolution. Scholars have used many approaches, on the whole with little success. Sometimes the answers to the questions posed do not give a clear or unambiguous indication of agriculture's role; sometimes the question cannot be answered from existing evidence. The greatest weakness of present approaches, however, is that most not only fail to distinguish phases of agrarian change but are incapable of doing so.

Let us first briefly explore the reasons why some questions now asked about agriculture fail to explain fully its role in the growth process. We must then take a more detailed look at the weakness of agricultural chronologies and the reasons for this weakness.

ASSESSING AGRICULTURES' ROLE

Whether agricultural change alone was sufficient to induce industrialization is not a question which should detain us, since it is agreed that no one factor could have caused the industrial revolution. A favourite question for academics is whether agricultural change was indispensable to the revolution. They assume that the answer will explain agriculture's role in Britain's transition; if the answer is positive (as it surely is) this will establish the importance of agriculture. This exercise, while clearly necessary, will only show agriculture as one amongst many indispensables. Therefore the answer is only a partial indication of agriculture's role in British growth. To say that agricultural progress was indispensable to Britain's growth does not sufficiently analyse its contribution to the mechanics of that growth.

Other studies try to assess agriculture's role by examining its various economic contributions: to capital for manufacturing industry and social overhead capital; to the supply of foodstuffs and raw materials; and to the demand situation, especially demand for commercially-produced manufactured goods. An immediate difficulty is that in each case agriculture was not the only contributor. Thus, for example, merchants provided at least part of the capital for canals. No one has been able to assess the precise extent of the agrarian community's contribution in any of these fields. Moreover, even precise figures would not allow us to distinguish between two very different roles for agricultural change: as a major stimulus to growth or, alternatively, as a response to the growth of the economy.

There are eminent advocates both for the view that agriculture was an exogenous stimulus and for the view that it simply responded to new opportunities created by general economic growth.[1] A decision on this issue rests partly upon comparative chronology; but the chronology of agricultural change is most uncertain in our period. Even the resolution of this issue may not be enough. If we decide that agriculture did provide an initial stimulus to growth, as A. H. John[2] tells us, it is still necessary to decide why other elements in the economy reacted to the stimulus in the way they did. Moreover, as we saw when we were discussing lag analysis, a short-run relationship does not establish the continuing relationship of agriculture to the growth of the economy. Agriculture could have provided an initial economic stimulus—through the effects of the good harvests in the 1730s and 1740s—but have been itself led into more fundamental changes by the economic growth which followed. There is no reason to assume that the boom in agricultural output in the 1740s was a sufficient stimulus for either the surge of economic growth after 1780 or the agrarian progress which accompanied it. Similarly, if agricultural change *was* a precondition for industrialization, we cannot assume automatically that the relationship between agricultural change and economic growth ceased to be important once industrialization had begun.

Alternatively, even if we were convinced that agricultural change was simply a response to general economic growth, some fundamental questions would be unanswered: in particular *why* agriculture responded and whether the response was quick enough to avoid a damper on economic growth. Agriculture is a notoriously conservative sector. If, indeed, it responded so well to the challenge of economic growth in the eighteenth century, what were the origins of this agrarian viability; when and in what circumstances did the viability emerge? The recent history of underdeveloped countries should be sufficient warning against assuming that agriculture will automatically adjust to a speed-up in the growth of the economy.

It is important to remember that agricultural progress was essentially part of a mechanism of change. Its place in this mechanism is not fully

[1] A. H. John, 1965; T. S. Ashton, 1955, p. 47; H. J. Habakkuk, 1965a.
[2] A. H. John, 1965.

exposed by the questions usually asked; we need to trace the continuing part played by agriculture over the whole transition period. The most precise way of doing this would be through the mathematical analysis of the development economists, which seeks to set out the quantitative interrelationships in the economy over time. This depends upon whether adequate data are available. Moreover, its usefulness would depend upon whether the method would take account of non-economic changes. At present these two qualifications are so important that it is difficult to see much benefit from the method. There seems more to gain from a more rigorous application of the methods of historians, by the accepted historical techniques of tracing the chronology of agricultural change, comparing this with change in other sectors of the economy and trying to assess what factors influenced the history of agricultural change.

However, a much more rigorous approach than is found in present agricultural histories is required, in the sense that a much greater effort is required to delineate phases of change and to distinguish their relative importance. I assume:

(a) that agricultural progress was an essential aspect of the British industrial revolution;

(b) that while it may have acted as a major stimulus at some stages in British history its principal importance was as an integral part of the growth mechanism over a long period of time. Perhaps we may also assume that:

(c) that it did respond to growth, but certainly not only the growth of the classic industrial revolution.

A BRITISH 'AGRARIAN REVOLUTION'?

On the assumption of agriculture's importance in the mechanism of change we will try to trace its history—when it changed, and the factors which influenced its rate of change. The historian will immediately reply that these are familiar questions. But how far have we succeeded in answering them?

The query arises because historians seem to have devoted enormous energies to explaining something which is not adequately established. Was there in fact, some time before 1780, a unique growth of agriculture which we refer to as the 'agricultural revolution'? Admittedly some historians prefer to be more cautious and refer only to a rapid growth of agriculture—not a revolution. Nevertheless, they still imply that the pace or depth of change was unique. But it has not been shown conclusively that what happened was unique; and, just as important, the timing of this change has received little attention.

Moreover, it is often not clear whether the historian has a narrow or broad view in mind: a change in technique or in the land-holding system may be significant for agricultural society, but not for production and the productivity of the whole country. What exactly is an agricultural revolution? I argue that none of the indicators historians use demonstrate that a revolutionary change occurred at this or any other time. Indeed, I claim that the traditional indicators are incapable of distinguishing a revolutionary phase or even of demonstrating marked improvements in growth rates.

Let us begin by looking at a general treatment of agricultural change in a recent influential work. Chambers and Mingay[3] hold that the difference between the agricultural revolution after 1750 and the preceding period was partly a difference of scale and partly of methodology. If 'scale' means the rate of growth of production we can agree that there was *probably* an increase in the rate of growth, but then agriculture in the seventeenth century had advanced more rapidly than earlier, which Chambers and Mingay admit. They say that the advance of the seventeenth and early eighteenth century was of 'supreme importance; but it was a condition rather than a fulfilment of the promise of agricultural revolution'.[4] The elegance of expression should not blind us to the lack of argument or evidence in support; and we are not told how to set about drawing the distinction implied. The sentence is, of course, only sound if you have been persuaded already. The same strictures would apply if 'scale' means the rate of technical innovation. No doubt the rate was higher in the late eighteenth century than in the late seventeenth century; but an increase in the rate of growth of technical innovation, or of production, is not in itself an adequate criteria for distinguishing a 'revolution'. Chambers and Mingay imply this themselves when they argue that the increased rate of growth of agriculture in the seventeenth century does not mean that there was an agricultural revolution at that time. Perhaps they believe that a further rise in the rate of growth in the eighteenth century pulled agriculture across a critical threshold rate of growth, above which an agricultural revolution was achieved. D. C. Coleman has argued persuasively against the idea of a threshold rate of growth above which a revolution occurs and below which it does not.[5]

The second aspect of their definition is even more obscure. Indeed, one cannot be sure what they mean by methodology since they admit elsewhere that scientific farming was not a feature of the British agrarian scene until the 1840s.[6]

[3] J. D. Chambers and G. E. Mingay, 1966, p. 13.
[4] *Ibid.*, p. 12.
[5] D. C. Coleman, 1956.
[6] J. D. Chambers and G. E. Mingay, 1966, p. 14.

Elsewhere in the book they make more specific approaches of a traditional kind to the measuring of agrarian change, but apparently they do not feel compelled to argue their general definition closely, nor to marshall evidence in support of this definition. Is the meaning and timing of the 'agricultural revolution' as well agreed as this would suggest? Of course it is not. Nor do we alter the problem significantly by substituting the more guarded phraseology. What is the evidence that in the second half of the eighteenth century there was '. . . an elaboration and generalization of principles already practised by the most progressive farmers in the first half of the eighteenth century'?[7] We are reminded that the problem is not so much to measure the beginning of change but to distinguish phases of change. Agrarian historians are remarkably unconvincing in distinguishing one phase of agrarian change from another.

Recently Dr. Eric Kerridge has argued passionately for a redating of the agricultural revolution,[8] placing it between 1540 and 1700, but again his thesis is inadequately established. His argument rests heavily upon the 'immense superiority' of ley (or up-and-down) farming, and his claims for it are impressive: 'All told, it is difficult to resist the conclusion that yields rose up to tenfold and fivefold on the average.[9] Since he claims that by 1660 it had replaced old systems on half the farmland, the effects of this one improvement must have been astonishing, and in addition there were floating water-meadows, large-scale marsh drainage, new fallow crops and grasses, improved manuring and stock breeding and other improvements.[10] However, it is clear that the five to tenfold increase is only a potential performance in more or less ideal circumstances, and Kerridge himself is at pains to show the variations in the advantage of up-and-down farming according to soil and other conditions.[11] Furthermore, the evidence that up-and-down farming had indeed penetrated half the farmland is not convincing, the more so because, to the reader, Dr. Kerridge is not altogether clear about what he means by 'up-and-down' husbandry. For instance, he claims that the transformation of the Vale of Pickering as a result of up-and-down husbandry was 'more thorough-going and revolutionary than even in the Midland Plain.' But, by his own account, the farming methods in the Vale of Pickering do not conform to his definition of up-and-down-husbandry: the farmers in the Vale kept tillage going until pasture was needed, and usually preceded a wheat crop with bare fallow, so that it might take twenty years to re-establish a full grass

[7] H. O. Meredith, 1958, p. 233.
[8] E. Kerridge, 1967.
[9] *Ibid.*, p. 331.
[10] *Ibid.*, p. 40.
[11] *Ibid.*, pp. 303 ff.

crop.[12] Where is the regular and restricted tillage aimed at preserving the turf in the soil throughout, so that the second year after the cessation of cultivation the sward was back almost to peak condition? Where is the eschewing of fallow stirrings which make recovery of the sward slow and inferior?[13]

Moreover, if the increase in production were as large as Kerridge claims, there probably should have been a substantial fall in prices. It is established that the cost of foodstuffs rose more than wages in this period.[14] Although Nef has argued that this has been exaggerated,[15] he still acknowledges the fact, which is the reverse of what we might expect if improvement were as spectacular as Kerridge postulates. True, meat prices rose less rapidly than grain, which is what would be expected from Kerridge's argument that the main influence of up-and-down methods was upon meat production. But even meat prices apparently rose more than wages,[16] which suggests that the improvement was not as pervasive and effective as Kerridge believes. Production probably rose, but surely less quickly than population if prices are a guide.

For comparative purposes a more interesting claim is that the spurt of production between 1540 and 1700 was 'quite unmatched' between 1750 and 1880. He argues forcefully that agriculture was able to feed a population which doubled between 1540 and 1700 and at the same time produce a growing export surplus of grain. By contrast, the later period saw massive imports of grain, which by 1850 were accounting for one quarter of flour consumed. However, the position was not as simple as Kerridge leads us to believe. If population doubled in the 160 years after 1540, it more than trebled in the 100 years after 1750. If we accept with Kerridge that a quarter of the population was fed by foreign imports of grain in 1851, this still means that wheat production in England and Wales was sufficient to support perhaps $13\frac{1}{2}$ million people in that year. In 1751, taking account of exports, it was feeding less than 7 million. The number of people fed by domestic grain production had almost doubled in the space of 100 years—a rate of growth more than twice the growth represented in the doubling of production during Dr. Kerridge's 160 year 'revolution'. A simple extension of his own arithmetic does more for his opponents than for him. Moreover, in the later period the proportion of population engaged in agriculture fell considerably, making its performance even more impressive; but there is no suggestion of a fall of a similar magnitude

[12] *Ibid.*, pp. 214–15.
[13] *Ibid.*, pp. 200–1.
[14] Y. S. Brenner, 1961–2 and 1962–3.
[15] J. U. Nef, 1937, pp. 155–85.
[16] *Ibid.*, p. 166.

in the earlier period. The main outlines of Kerridge's arguments do not stand up to critical examination.

Let us return to consider the methodology which historians have used to 'prove' an agricultural revolution. Traditional approaches have used enclosure and technical improvements as a measure of progress, occasionally modified by an analysis of the changing nature of the agrarian community, and the form of land holding and occupation. More recently Deane and Cole have attempted some interesting production estimates for the eighteenth century.

We know that enclosure had been proceeding for centuries before the eighteenth century: but we are convinced that it was much more rapid in the eighteenth century following the new form of enclosure by private Act of Parliament. Parliamentary enclosure has been adequately traced, and 1750–60 was the beginning of a rapid increase in its rate.[17] Does this indicate the beginning of the agricultural revolution? There are many reasons for believing that it is not an adequate indication. The first and simplest reason is that enclosure affected only a proportion of agricultural land. We know that in 1700 some half of the cultivated area of England had already been enclosed or had never known open field cultivation.[18] Therefore enclosure is an irrelevant measure of improvement for half of farming in what is generally agreed to be the vital period. Furthermore, parliamentary enclosure may not be representative of all enclosure. Clearly there were important enclosures by agreement prior to, and probably concurrent with, the early stages of parliamentary enclosure (in the 1740s and 1750s). Chambers and Mingay go so far as to suggest that the amount of land affected was half that affected by parliamentary enclosure.[19] The chronology and extent of enclosure by agreement is not nearly so well known as that of parliamentary enclosure. One can only guess at the overall pattern which might emerge if it were possible to combine both forms of enclosure in a single index.

Therefore it may be a mistake to assume that the sharp upsurge of parliamentary enclosure after 1750 was a break in the trend; it may have been only a fluctuation in the rate of enclosure, being simply a reflection of enclosure's response to the state of the market and other conditions. Such fluctuations were experienced later: enclosure was attractive when grain prices rose after the late 1740s: but when climbing prices slackened in the 1780s and early 1790s so did the rate of enclosure; when grain prices soared during the French Wars the rate of enclosure jumped higher than ever. Such relationships may also have

[17] Phyllis Deane and W. A. Cole, 1962, p. 94.
[18] J. D. Chambers and G. E. Mingay, 1966, p. 77.
[19] *Ibid.*, p. 78. See also W. G. Hoskins, 1955.

held true for the period before 1750. Perhaps the period of uncertain grain prices in the 1730s and 1740s provided little incentive to enclosure, so that enclosure was less attractive than it had been and was to become. These decades perhaps represent a temporary lag in a movement which began earlier through agreement and Chancery and which resumed later at an increasing rate using a different medium. Our lack of knowledge of enclosure by agreement, both its extent and timing, precludes a categoric conclusion that the decade 1750–60 was the beginning of a new era of enclosure, unless we are content to look only at parliamentary enclosure.

Even if we could measure the incidence of enclosure accurately, and even if we agreed in interpreting the figures, we could still be short of a solution because of the various relationships which enclosure could have to other agricultural improvements. Enclosure may have been undertaken specifically to permit technical improvement—so that a direct and positive connection existed. Alternatively, it may have been adopted only when the open field became a clear barrier to the adoption of further technical improvements. Here 'improvement' precedes enclosure by some margin. Or there may have been no relationship: as Clapham has said, 'some of the "old enclosed regions" were as intensely conservative as any in the kingdom'.[20] There may have been—indeed there were—a variety of relationships between enclosure and technical improvements. In some counties, such as Oxfordshire, enclosure would be a hopeless measure of agricultural advance. Havinden[21] believes that improved crop rotations were widely used there in the late seventeenth century, but of course Oxford was one of the last bastions of the open field.

It may be argued that the weaknesses in regarding enclosure as an indicator of change are weaknesses of insufficient knowledge and that these gaps may be filled by further research, particularly the detailed regional studies recently so popular. Up to a point this is obviously so—we may expect to fill out our knowledge of enclosure by agreement and through Chancery. We may also expect to discover more about the relationship between enclosure and other improvements, though it may be doubted whether generality will be found in the latter relationship (and there also remains the question of whether regional studies set out to provide this knowledge). However, we can never escape the irrelevance of enclosure as an indicator of improvement in the major areas already enclosed in 1700.

The difficulties and problems of using enclosure as an indication of the agrarian revolution involve the historian in a great dilemma because

[20] J. H. Clapham, 1957, p. 219.
[21] M. A. Havinden, 1961.

it is obvious that it *was* part of improving agriculture: enclosure made a unique and important contribution to the changing agrarian scene, and therefore it is an indispensable wing of the traditional approach. The other wing—the technical changes of the agrarian revolution—produces a similar dilemma. The difficulty here is to produce a satisfactory measurement of improved technique. At one time historians were content with tracing the initial innovation of new techniques, and this still occupies the attention of some. Most now would regard the approach as inadequate, arguing that what we need to know is when these techniques came to be applied on a wide scale.

In discussing technical change on a wide scale, writers often give the impression that they are making a direct study of technical improvements: they refer to the rapid extension of the use of fodder crops, the adoption of four-course rotation, of improved breeds of animal, improved farm implements and equipment, marling and so on. But a direct measure of technical improvement is historically and theoretically impossible. There is no known way of combining these various factors in any comprehensible way. We can devise no common denominator for all of these various factors.

The problem is a problem of weighting; and a careful statement of some of its intricacies reveals the impossibility of the task. First, there were a variety of new fodder crops, and since the spread of these crops was not parallel we must devise a way of combining them to get a single index. This is perhaps not an insuperable problem—the acreage of each, together with some adjustment for the productivity of the various crops, might give a reasonable indication. But how do we allow for the differences of purpose which the same crop served in different regions? Clover and turnip could be used as a substitute for fallow on a heavy soil farm and this would affect productivity. But on a farm in Norfolk these crops were part of a rotation system which transformed land use. The sum of their individual effects was nowhere near the effect when all were applied in systematic rotation. And of course there could be a third case where the fodder crop was inserted into an expanded rotation system which still included fallow.[22] Do we assume that these variations have no importance?

An even more intractable problem is the weighting of disparate technical advances. How do we compare the effects of planting clover with the effects of improved drainage, better implements, the substitution of horses for oxen, improved breeds of stock, marling, greater use of fertilizers, the spread of four-course rotation and flexible rotation systems? Even if we had perfect knowledge of the incidence of each of these we could not combine them satisfactorily. If there were complete

[22] M. A. Havinden, 1961, pp. 77–9.

stagnation and then change we might be able to cope reasonably well, but this was not so in Britain. I emphasize that this is more than a problem of inadequate historical data. Even in current studies the contribution of technical improvement is assumed to be the residue after eliminating other influences on agricultural production.[23] It seems quite hopeless to look for a satisfactory direct measurement of technical improvement. Where historians attempt to do so their judgements can be no more than impressions. This can hardly be convincing to the outsider since historians' impressions differ markedly.

Alternatively, historians have used indirect measures, assessing the incidence of agricultural writings advocating improved techniques: tracing the 'popularity' of agrarian issues. This is a legitimate historical technique, but in this case of doubtful value. The relationship of agricultural writings to practice may not be as direct as we would like. One of the assumptions of this approach is that the writings of the Tulls, Marshalls and Youngs provided a lead which persuaded the majority of farmers to better methods; but exactly how long this persuasion took is a matter of conjecture. And perhaps the lead came from the opposite direction—practising farmers finally convincing the writers—as in Hampshire where Jones tells us: 'At the end of the eighteenth century agriculturalists still claimed to be convinced of the necessity of the sheep-fold. Much of this acclaim was retrospective and was prompted by the decline of the old folding system brought about by the vast conversion of sheep-walk to tillage';[24] or as Mr. Trow-Smith argues of medieval farmers: 'They learnt by example and observation; and, mercifully, did not read the text-books, which lagged hopelessly behind current practice.'[25] Finally, if it is not possible to devise a common denominator for studying techniques directly, may it not be a delusion to suppose we can devise a common denominator of this indirect kind? Can we in fact provide a comprehensive test of the interest of the rural community in improvement? An interest in crop rotation in Norfolk does not necessarily indicate an interest in better farm implements or improved breeds in Nottingham, or even in Norfolk; and surely it is just as difficult to assess the practical significance of a reference to improved breeds combined with two references to clover in rotation as to combine these things directly in a technological index. A well-established textbook generalization emphasizes the growing popularity of improvement in the eighteenth century; but an eminent historian argues precisely the same case for the seventeenth century.[26] Who is right? There is simply no way of telling.

[23] See E. D. Domar, 1961.
[24] E. L. Jones, 1960, p. 10.
[25] R. Trow-Smith, 1957. Quote by Joan Thirsk in *Agricultural History Review VI*, 1958, p. 54.   [26] C. Wilson, 1965, Ch. 7.

Even a superficial reading of the academic literature makes it clear that we provide no guidelines for anyone to judge for themselves. Examine, for example, some recent judgements about British agriculture by professional historians,[27] and ask whether it is possible to disentangle the results.

'. . . the rigidities imposed by the manorial system were shattered by . . . the Black Death.' (Chambers and Mingay).

In the period 1540–1640 there was 'no major technical transition'. (E. L. Jones) But in the same period '. . . a powerful impetus was given to the forces that were working for commercialization of agriculture in England at large' and 'Suburban farming was revolutionized' (F. J. Fisher).

'. . . evidence abounds that a critical, improving spirit of curiosity and experiment was abroad, even in the first half of the [seventeenth] century.' (C. Wilson).

'. . . if the peasant of Henry VIII's day could have returned [to the late seventeenth century] . . . he would have felt at home.' (W. G. Hoskins).

'Between the middle of the seventeenth century and the middle of the eighteenth century, English agriculture underwent a transformation in its techniques out of all proportion to the rather limited widening of its market.' (E. L. Jones).

'. . . departure from traditional practice marks a new agricultural epoch, and its acceleration in the second half of the eighteenth century in the form of the classical enclosure movement and the first unmistakable steps of the agricultural pioneers towards "high farming", mark the opening of the Agricultural Revolution.' (Chambers and Mingay).

But in the middle of the nineteenth century we are told of '. . . the conservatism and ignorance of most farmers' and that most farmers were '. . . incapable of altering or adapting their practice': they were '. . . a race of bucolic robots' (McGregor).

Each of these statements has its own nuance of meaning, but is it really possible to reconcile them? And if they are not reconcilable, who is right and who is wrong? When the basis of each argument is examined and compared with the others, surely none is convincing. Not only are their indicators inadequate to support the conclusions, but there is little effort to develop a comparative methodology. Perhaps agriculture did change rapidly in period y but did it change more rapidly than in other periods? And did it have more profound implica-

[27] J. D. Chambers and G. E. Mingay, 1966, p. 5; E. L. Jones, 1965, p. 64; F. J. Fisher, 1935, p. 64; C. Wilson, 1965, p. 28; W. G. Hoskins, 1957, p. 190; E. L. Jones, 1965, p. 1; J. D. Chambers and G. E. Mingay, 1966, p. 4; Lord Ernle, 1961, introduction by O. R. McGregor, pp. cxvi, cxviii.

tions for the rest of the economy? Traditional methodology is unable to cope with such questions.

All this is not to argue that studies of enclosure and technical improvement are pointless. No doubt they do contribute to our knowledge of how a particular increase in production was achieved. But alone they cannot demonstrate that there was an increase of production significantly departing from previous trends, nor show accurately the timing of growth in agriculture; these must be shown by other means.

Two other indicators may be dealt with briefly. The first is the changing pattern of occupational distribution, demonstrating the ability of agriculture to sustain a larger and larger non-agricultural workforce. This meets the seemingly insuperable barriers of the rural character of much industry before the industrial revolution and of part-time involvement in agriculture.[28] There may be no way of determining the precise extent of the agrarian workforce in the period before factory industry—at least not on a national level—and at intervals frequent enough for our purpose.

Changes in the size of the typical unit of cultivation may be a further indicator. This is partly associated with the decline of feudal relationships and partly with enclosure.[29] Undoubtedly it is necessary to trace changing farm sizes to tell the full story of the development of agriculture, but few would be prepared to settle the problem of dating on this basis. The relationship between farm size and other production variables is too indirect and tenuous to be sure of any constancy.

EIGHTEENTH-CENTURY PRODUCTION ESTIMATES

Deane and Cole's recent work on agriculture uses new methods and revises old conclusions. This work is important less for its conclusions than for its methodology, which—though it can be criticized—is at least a departure from the 'impossible' techniques of traditional studies. They make a direct effort to estimate production trends. While their methods have serious weaknesses, which we will now consider, it is important to remember that their break from traditional methods is essential and timely.

Their methods of estimating meat production are interesting and ingenious, particularly their novel use of excise figures of skins and hides. However, there are two major weaknesses in their technique, both of which tend to understate the growth of meat production in eighteenth-century Britain.

[28] A. J. and R. H. Tawney, 1934–5.
[29] For a summary see G. E. Mingay, 1963a.

First, they assume a constant relationship between the weight of hides and meat; but an animal of larger size will increase meat weight proportionally more than the increase in hide weight—just as the volume in a watertank increases proportionally more than the area of its walls and ends. Historians believe that the average size of animals increased in the eighteenth century,[30] so the increase in the weight of hides is likely to understate the growth of meat production. We may add in parenthesis that the weight of hides varies considerably between different breeds of animal, and this too could be a source of variation between hide and meat weights if the breed of the typical farm animal was changing, as it almost certainly was.

Secondly, they ignore the reduction of bone and offal which they note elsewhere[31] as the likely consequence of improved breeding over the century. This may have been of particular importance because of the diminishing use of plough-oxen. The hides of plough-oxen are presumably included in the excise figures, but even if their meat were consumed on the farm they would probably not have supplied as much meat as an animal of similar size raised primarily for its flesh, and of course this also ignores the question of quality. Draught animals tended to be bigger than average, so their contribution to hide weight would be proportionally higher than their numbers.

Perhaps the most unfortunate aspect of these calculations is that they begin only in the 1720s. At first sight this appears to be early enough, because the index remains more or less on a plateau till the early 1750s and then begins a steady climb. The difficulty is that the cattle plague of the 1740s and early 1750s disturbs the series. We cannot dismiss the possibility that the upward trend had begun sometime earlier, to be temporarily disturbed by the losses from the cattle plague.

Their second main section on agricultural output concerns corn production. Their method assumes that consumption varied directly with population, an assumption dangerous in the short run (which they recognize) and unproven in the long run.

Recently a number of writers have argued that the beginning of the agricultural revolution should be pushed back into the seventeenth century. These writers have mounted a more serious challenge to traditional dating than ever before, though they are far from establishing their case. They also raise issues which the approach used by Deane and Cole is unable to handle. It is suggested, for example, that increased output after the Restoration meant growing per capita consumption, and was reflected in falling prices. This argument, of course, challenges Deane and Cole's assumptions about corn consumption per capita.

[30] G. E. Fussell, 1929; Phyllis Deane and W. A. Cole, 1962, pp. 69–70.
[31] *Ibid.*, p. 70.

While there is little direct evidence of rising consumption standards, the history of grain prices up to 1740 would certainly allow of such a possibility.

This view has been reinforced by the conclusions of E. L. Jones and A. H. John.[32] While their work suffers from the weakness of relying too heavily upon a traditional approach, there is nevertheless enough in their thesis to raise doubts about the assumptions of Deane and Cole. Jones and John look at British agriculture on a regional basis and decide that the extension of arable farming on the light soils dates from the late seventeenth century. They argue that this caused growing pressure upon the traditional arable areas, which were unable to compete because they did not have the same margin for improvement. There are two principal points of interest for us in this hypothesis. One is that the improvement on light soils took place earlier than we are accustomed to believe, and the other that it caused a readjustment of agriculture in the Midlands. Neither thesis is satisfactorily established. True, Jones refers to evidence that turnip and clover were introduced earlier than we imagined, and he shows that their use was geographically widespread; but some of the examples he gives are of garden rather than field use. More important, there is little evidence to show that they were used by a significant proportion of farmers throughout Britain even on light soils.

There can be no doubt about the marked increase in sheep numbers; nor would one disagree that price movements may indicate 'that supply did tend to pull just ahead of demand', but one may doubt whether this establishes his thesis. Strangely, the contemporary evidence about improvement which he cites is drawn mainly from the middle of the eighteenth century.[33] While one would hesitate to say that this interesting thesis is wrong, one may doubt that Jones has given sufficient evidence that 'the true transformation of crop rotations was accomplished with the adoption on a *significant scale* in the latter half of the seventeenth century of the innovations in fodder cropping'.[34]

His evidence about the early readjustment of clay belt agriculture is also inconclusive. He relies on evidence of a shift from arable to pasture in Leicestershire. There is little, however, to suggest a significant switch from arable to permanent pasture in the Midlands generally[35] —though there may have been a shift towards more extensive use of pasture in rotations.

[32] A. H. John, 1965; E. L. Jones, 1965.
[33] *Ibid.*, pp. 11, 12, 15.
[34] *Ibid.*, p. 5 (my italics).
[35] See W. G. Hoskins, 1957, Ch. X. Hoskins believes that the switch to pasture came only after enclosure—i.e. in the second half of the eighteenth century.

These ideas raise some important queries relevant to Deane and Cole's estimates. Was there a significant increase in animal products before the mid-eighteenth century? If there was rising production on lighter soils, and a switch to pasture on heavy soils, there may well have been such an increase. Deane and Cole hold that the value of grasslands and grain production were roughly equal at the beginning and the end of the century. However, it is more likely that grassland production increased more than grain. Beef production slightly lagged behind population increase and so did grain production, but mutton and wool production grew much more rapidly. Whereas population grew by 60 per cent over the century, wool production increased by some 135 per cent.[36] Moreover, the highest rate of increase was in the first forty years of the century.

The evidence on grassland production raises doubts about the basic assumptions underlying the Deane and Cole agricultural production estimates. They believe that average corn consumption per capita did not alter much over the century; but on rather dubious grounds they translate this into an assumption that total agricultural production varied with population—this despite their observation that: 'Probably the diet of ordinary people became more varied as a result of rising incomes.'[37] Perhaps consumption standards rose before 1750, as John believes.

In the light of these queries it is difficult to accept unequivocally the Deane and Cole hypothesis that the whole of agricultural production varied with corn, which in turn reflected principally the variations of population growth. But despite qualifications, the difficulties of traditional methods make estimates of this kind an important advance. A further interesting development is the promise of direct estimates from estate accounts.[38] At the moment, however, we are still faced with rather unsatisfactory data on production and productivity.

THE ATTITUDINAL BACKGROUND

The discussion so far has been mainly in traditional terms. There may be more subtle methodological problems involved which we should consider. Perhaps a measure of achievement, such as production or productivity, only partly explains how and why changes occurred—because the basis of these changes may be a prolonged evolution of new attitudes in the agrarian community.

[36] Phyllis Deane and W. A. Cole, 1962, p. 68.
[37] *Ibid.,* p. 64.
[38] E. L. Jones, 1967, p. 16n.

An exclusive concentration upon measures of achievement may well cause us to ignore an important dimension of agricultural change—the attitudinal dimension. Recent improvement efforts in traditional peasant societies surely demonstrate that new techniques, and even knowledge of new techniques, are not enough. The farmer must also be willing to apply or at least try these techniques. But modern functional models emphasize aggregate achievement, i.e. broad movements in production levels, ignoring the attitudinal background to these achievements.

Thus we find Kuznets emphasizing production aggregates, to the point of saying that agriculture will only alter significantly when industrialization is already under way. 'For any significant transformation of agriculture in the crowded traditional societies and any marked rise in overhead capital investment are, to my mind, already part and parcel of modern economic growth; and given the technological, economic, and social interrelations within the economy, can hardly occur unless they are *accompanied* by the changes that Professor Rostow assigns to the take-off stage.'[39]

The meaning of the passage depends of course upon what he means by such phrases as 'significant transformation', 'crowded traditional societies' and 'modern economic growth', but its sense is that agricultural change will be simultaneous with the growth of the economy generally. In the sense of a Keynesian income flow this must be true, but in a historical sense there can be quite fundamental changes in agriculture which are not reflected in the quantity of total production. Agriculture is notoriously conservative, especially in 'traditional' communities. If compulsion is not used (and even sometimes when it is) the farmer is slow to change, and a significant increase in production may indicate that a fundamental change in attitude had been brewing amongst farmers for some time. The point applies to all of the standards of measurement we have so far discussed because they are standards of achievement, and yet the base on which this achievement is built may be quite as 'revolutionary' as the achievement itself. The point is simply illustrated in the parliamentary enclosure movement. Its very existence represented a fundamental change in the attitude of the government (and one presumes of the community) compared with the attitudes of the Tudors and early Stuarts towards enclosure. The significance of parliamentary enclosure is not just that it removed a barrier to rapid change: it also represented a new view of the function and character of agriculture in the community—a view that had taken a long time to develop.[40] On a different level, the individual enclosure

[39] S. Kuznets, 1963, p. 37.
[40] See M. Beresford, 1961.

act may have been only the denouement of a gradual change in the thinking of the farmers belonging to a village.

We may look upon the adoption of new techniques in the same light. It may be exaggerating the case to say that they were only the means of translating a fundamental change in outlook into the achievement of increased production, but the exaggeration emphasizes a fundamental point: that the acceptance of new techniques is at least as important as the techniques themselves. The fact that improved techniques are available is no guarantee that they will be accepted by the farmers.

Is this an over-technical refinement? Is there likely to be a substantial delay between the time the farmer realizes the advantages of new techniques and when he applies them? If it is the young who are persuaded first there may be a delay of some few years until the young man inherits the family plot and can begin to put his exciting ideas into practice, but this is a relatively minor refinement. The real problem arises when the process of changing attitude is a creeping process—by gradual persuasion, perhaps by the example of a few innovators who inspire others to follow, others who in turn eventually persuade the timid majority to follow. If the process was of this kind, and it probably was, can we afford to ignore the early stages when the few were setting an example? This phase would not be reflected in overall figures but perhaps the example was an indispensable pre-condition for the large-scale changes which followed. Obviously we cannot ignore the innovators, because they were an essential part of the historical process whereby agriculture achieved a broad flexibility.

This seems to turn agricultural history back full circle: we are back to the point of looking at the great innovators, though of course we still need to trace the phase of rapid adoption. Nevertheless, we are still left with a dilemma: how we may define and put limits on the phase where attitudes were being conditioned. There had been innovators and improvers for centuries past—were they *all* indispensable to the changes of the 'agricultural revolution'? Was the spread of ley farming in the sixteenth and early seventeenth centuries, or the disruption to feudalism from the Black Death, part of this process? Here we are back to the old historical problem of linking causes. Obviously the isolated progressive is of no interest to us, nor is the progressive of an earlier time who had no connection with the changing attitudes we seek to explore. The distinction we must draw is between an improving farmer who was a leader of a newly emerging spirit of improvement, and one who was *not* directly linked to the new enterprising spirit, even though he may have established the conditions on which the expansion was built. Britain was no longer a feudal society in 1600, and this is important in understanding the history of the eighteenth century, because this was part of the scene into which the great improvements were injected. However, it is ludicrous to suggest that the changing attitudes of Oxfordshire farmers towards enclosure in the late eighteenth century were the direct result of the outbreak of Black Death in 1348. Moreover, the agricultural revolution could hardly be said to have relied on the impetus of the changes associated with the Black Death. European countries experienced the Black Death and ley farming, but there was no general agricultural revolution in Europe in the eighteenth century. We may therefore expect to find some additional positive factors in Britain which will explain the deviation. Whether we can isolate the attitudinal changes which led to the agricultural revolution remains to be seen, but I hope it is obvious that we must be prepared to make the effort, in addition to our efforts to be more accurate about the timing of the movement in production which followed. Efforts to improve our knowledge of production performance are vital—but it is also vital that we understand that the task of full explanation does not end there.

FURTHER READING

† CHAMBERS, J. D.: 'Enclosure and the Labour Supply in the Industrial Revolution'.
The Vale of Trent 1670–1800.
CHAMBERS, J. D. and MINGAY, G. E.: *The Agricultural Revolution 1750–1880.*
DEANE, PHYLLIS and COLE, W. A.: *British Economic Growth 1688–1959.*
* HABAKKUK, H. J.: 'Economic Functions of English Landowners in the Seventeenth and Eighteenth Centuries'.
*† HAVINDEN, M. A.: 'Agricultural Progress in Open-field Oxfordshire'.
HUNT, H. G.: 'Landownership and Enclosure 1750–1830'.
JOHN, A. H.: 'Aspects of English Economic Growth in the First Half of the Eighteenth Century'.
  * 'The Course of Agricultural Change 1660–1760'.
  † 'Agricultural Productivity and Economic Growth in England 1700–1760'.
JONES, E. L.: 'Eighteenth-Century Changes in Hampshire Chalkland Farming'.
  *† 'Agricultural and Economic Growth in England 1660–1750: Agricultural Change'.
KERRIDGE, E.: *The Agricultural Revolution.*
* MINGAY, G. E.: 'The "Agricultural Revolution" in English History: A Reconsideration'.

English Landed Society in the Eighteenth Century.

Enclosure and the Small Farmer in the Age of the Industrial Revolution.

PARKER, R. A. C.: 'Coke of Norfolk and the Agrarian Revolution'.

QUINT, M.: 'The Idea of Progress in an Iraqi Village'.

THIRSK, J.: 'Seventeenth-Century Agriculture and Social Change'.

TROW-SMITH, R.: *English Husbandry, from the Earliest Times to the Present Day.*

A History of British Livestock Husbandry 1700–1900.

WILSON, C.: *England's Apprenticeship 1603–1763.* (Ch. 7)

* Reprinted in W. E. Minchinton (ed.): *Essays in Agrarian History.*

† Reprinted in E. L. Jones (ed.): *Agriculture and Economic Growth in England 1650–1815.*

4 Population and Effective Demand

Historians have often puzzled over whether population growth was a cause or effect of the industrial revolution. It was probably both. If we take 'cause' to mean a positive influence upon the course of British economic growth in the eighteenth century, then population growth was probably a 'cause'. The growth of population must have stimulated demand and provided an essential, growing labour supply. On the other hand, the industrial revolution must surely have been a necessary condition of continued population growth, if not in the eighteenth century, certainly in the nineteenth. However, these answers to our 'cause or effect' questions are certainly not solutions to all our problems —they merely raise more complex problems.

In particular, two major questions arise from these answers. First, which economic elements were influenced by population growth, and what can be said about the nature and extent of this influence? Deane and Cole[1] discuss the effects of population growth upon demand and the labour supply, upon transport improvement, and upon the search for inventions and their commercial application. The latter are studies in themselves, because they were certainly significantly influenced by things other than population growth—the capacity for invention must have been increased by the scientific revolution, for example. If population growth did exert a decisive influence upon these factors, it would have been chiefly through the growth of demand. Therefore the first step in exploring these connections must be to decide the extent to which the growth of demand depended upon population growth. This may require an assessment of other influences on demand, such as the growth of foreign trade, changes in income levels or the distribution of income, or significant changes in taste. I cannot pretend to discuss all of these, as each is a major study in itself. However, we may look in general terms at the first question, the relationship between population growth and demand—a seminal question which has received far too little attention. We will examine this problem and the various issues surrounding it in the first half of this chapter.

1 Phyllis Deane and W. A. Cole, 1962, esp. pp. 88 ff.

The second major problem which this chapter discusses is whether population growth was exogenous—and *if* it was exogenous, *when* it was. The current view seems to be that continued population growth after 1780 depended upon economic progress. Before that date, between 1740 and 1780, population grew mainly because of a falling death-rate which fell for no very obvious reason—perhaps it was purely fortuitous, and there is certainly little evidence that it fell for economic reasons. Therefore most historians would argue that the initial upward movement of population in the eighteenth century was exogenous. But, as we shall see, it is possible to reach very different conclusions by using different assumptions in interpreting the figures.

POPULATION AND DEMAND MOVEMENTS IN EIGHTEENTH-CENTURY BRITAIN

Deane and Cole have the most comprehensive recent treatment of the relationship between demand and population growth. Broadly they argue that movements in demand coincided with population movements, though of course their arguments in support are much more subtle than such a brief summary would imply.

It must be admitted that this part of their book is far from clear, and since the meaning of what they say has been disputed, I should pause to give an admittedly personal interpretation of their work.[2] On the demand side what they appear to say is as follows. In the first half of the century, harvest fluctuations had pronounced effects upon agricultural prices because population growth was low. When yields were high, prices fell and real incomes of wage-earners improved, but the real incomes of the farmers declined (though their hired labourers benefited because labour was required to gather the good harvest). When harvests were poor the inelastic demand for foodstuffs pushed food prices up disproportionately, to the benefit of the farming community and the detriment of the real incomes of wage-earners. They argue, too, that demand from farmers was the most important element in the domestic market for manufactured goods in the first half of the century. Therefore the market was expanding most rapidly in times of rising food prices.

They then use these ideas to explain in detail how the expansion of the economy was limited by restricted demand in the first half of the century, and how this restriction was lifted by population growth after 1750. In the first half of the century low population growth had two

[2] The relevant part of Deane and Cole is at pp. 80–95. What follows is an abbreviated version of A. G. Thompson, 1966.

important consequences. First, there were countervailing influences at work upon domestic demand for industrial goods, since the welfare of the farmers and wage-earners tended to fluctuate inversely. If the farmers improved their position (as a result of rising food prices) the result was dampened by the fact that this involved a fall in the purchasing power of wage-earners (even if the effect on balance was to raise industrial demand). Second, there was a tendency towards an inverse fluctuation of agricultural and industrial production. Food prices would normally rise only when harvests were poor in such a stagnant market. Even though rising prices meant growing industrial demand (from farmers), '. . . there is no reason to assume that the increased demand for industrial goods more than offset the loss in agricultural output'.[3] On the other hand, good harvests would be offset by a decline in the rate of growth of industrial demand as a result of falling demand from farmers—whose incomes sank as food prices fell. Deane and Cole are thus able to show how the low rate of population growth retarded the growth of the economy in the first half of the eighteenth century.

Population was expanding rapidly in the second half of the century, and '. . . since the agricultural community was thus assured of an expanding market for its produce, the significance of harvest variations began to change.'[4] In their view this change had two aspects: rising food prices could now be experienced even when harvests were good, and rising food prices were no longer a necessary prerequisite for the growth of demand for industrial goods.

They do not see the change in 'the significance of harvest variations' as a complete reversal of the earlier situation. Rising food prices still brought growth of effective demand; but there is still a fundamental difference from periods of rising prices earlier in the century, because now rising food prices could occur even when harvests were good. They are trying to show how the growth of population altered the situation in which the agricultural community could enjoy high or rising returns. In this new situation high food prices and relatively buoyant industrial demand were no longer the corollary of poor harvests, while good harvests no longer meant plummeting food prices. The countervailing forces of the first forty years of the century were no longer as significant. Deane and Cole are thus able to explain why the growth of the economy was so much greater after 1743 than it had been before that date.

One of the principal difficulties about the Deane and Cole analysis is that they make no *specific* analysis of changes in the nature of demand over the century. There was clearly some significant change because they argue that in the second half of the eighteenth century, in contrast

[3] Phyllis Deane and W. A. Cole, 1962, p. 92.   [4] *Ibid.*, p. 94.

to the first half, the economy grew *most* rapidly when food prices were rising relatively slowly. This implies that demand for industrial goods no longer depended primarily upon farmers. Apparently they believe that when food prices rose, farmers diverted the increases of income into investment, and: 'There is no evidence that this wave of investment directly stimulated industrial demand.'[5] But if industrial demand did not rest so heavily upon farmers, upon whom did it rest? Perhaps upon foreign purchasers? But according to the Deane and Cole view, the main purchasers of British products had their purchasing powers limited by British demand for their goods, so that the demand situation was basically determined within Britain (see Chapter 6). Was there a growing demand from the lower classes? We are not told, and here lies the most significant weakness in Deane and Cole's treatment. This is strange when we realize that it is almost axiomatic that industrialization implies a large demand for mass-produced goods from the bulk of the population. The industrial country is one which produces industrial goods commercially for the overwhelming bulk of the population. The lower classes no longer depend on making their own clothes, utensils and furniture. In Britain the question is not whether this happened but *when* it happened, and this is surely a pertinent question for the eighteenth century. Deane and Cole do not consider the question, which is a serious omission. Clearly they imply that the nature of commercial demand did not change significantly until 1750 at least. Yet there is considerable evidence that there was such a change.

A. H. John[6] believes that expansion of demand began early in the eighteenth century before the growth of population had begun. In John's view agricultural improvement touched off this expansion by lowering the price of basic foodstuffs, thus releasing purchasing power for other agricultural and industrial products. In direct contrast to Deane and Cole, John argues that the rising demand for commercially-produced industrial products came from the lower classes as their food costs fell early in the century. This is obviously an important issue in any review of demand movements.

It is possible to have considerable sympathy with John's idea but nevertheless to believe that he has taken it too far. Thus he tries to establish a case for general economic advance on a broad front, despite the fact that there is little evidence of this in the first forty years of the century. There is some evidence of regional advance, particularly in manufacturing, though this may have been offset by difficulties for the farming community in general. John does argue with some force that the main indicators which we rely upon (trade figures and population)

---

[5] Phyllis Deane and W. A. Cole, 1962, p. 95.
[6] A. H. John, 1965 and 1961.

are not acceptable in the situation, but this of course does not establish the converse of what those indicators show.

Apart from his direct evidence of industrial advance, which appears to be limited to particular regions, his main argument rests on the proposition that overall demand would have risen. This in turn rests upon his efforts to show that demand of the farmers would not have fallen, despite falling prices in the face of stagnant demand. In short, he is arguing against Deane and Cole's 'countervailing forces' idea, at least in times of falling food prices. If consumption of farmers did not fall, and if wage-earners increased their purchases of other items as basic foodstuffs fell in price, overall demand must have risen. John is unconvincing in his view that farmers did not restrict consumption as their incomes fell.

John supposes that E. L. Jones[7] supports this interpretation because Jones believes that investment in agriculture did not fall during depression. But there is no reason why this should mean that incomes and consumption were not falling at such times, as John assumes. Jones writes that landlords became 'comparatively insensitive to poor financial returns',[8] implying, of course, that investment was undertaken *despite* falling income. Later in his article Jones hypothesizes that agrarian change in the late seventeenth and early eighteenth centuries may have reduced the incomes of small farmers, and increased the incomes of the successful innovators, particularly on light soils, so that the net effect was 'the concentration of incomes in fewer hands, with implications for the ratio of basic to luxury goods purchased',[9] a proposition which hardly supports the John argument.

John makes more convincing use of the evidence of increasing sheep numbers in the period, though we have yet to be shown the net effect on farmers' incomes of rising sheep numbers, together with falling grain prices and an unknown movement in total grain production. Also, as John recognizes, the rise of sheep numbers may reflect regional variation in growth. On the light soil belt it probably indicates growing wealth. But in the clay belts the conversions to pasture, which Jones mentions as being the consequence of light soil competition in grains, can hardly indicate rising prosperity. On the contrary, the clay farmer's income would probably have been under pressure if the conversion had been forced. Moreover, we must remember that the significant point under discussion is income available for consumption, not simply income. If sheep numbers were growing rapidly this must have represented a substantial investment. The rising income of light soil farmers

[7] E. L. Jones, 1965.
[8] *Ibid.*, p. 9.
[9] *Ibid.*, pp. 16–17.

may not have meant a similar rise in consumption, if part of that income was going into building up herds. Similarly, if the clay-belt farmers were being forced to switch to pasture farming, as Jones suggests, their consumption may have been squeezed even more than their income. Therefore the rise in the consumption of the lightsoil farmers may not have offset the falling consumption of the heavysoil farmers. The investment in herds may not have had immediate multiplier effects if they were built up internally on the farm, and the immediate economic stimulus may have been small, particularly if agricultural incomes were being redistributed in a way that was unfavourable to consumer spending.

Thus it appears that John has overstated his case for a general advance in industrial demand and in the economy in the first half of the eighteenth century. Nevertheless, there *is* evidence supporting his important proposition of increasing social depth to industrial demand, although the overall effect was probably limited, and the advance which took place appears to be regional.

John finds indication of greater depth of demand in an increase in the consumption of tea, sugar, and tobacco, but there must be some doubt about the extent of lower-class demand for these products at this stage. More relevant is his evidence of increased consumption of linens and printed calicos, and growing production of cheap household pottery; and there is also evidence of growth in the Yorkshire woollen industry and Lancashire textiles in this period. It is of some significance, perhaps, that most of his examples come from the North-west of England.

Other evidence supports the idea of increased demand in the period. Phyllis Deane's estimates of wool textile output suggest growth of some 42 per cent between 1695 and 1740.[10] This was about equally shared between the domestic market and exports;[11] between 1700–01 and 1740–41 domestic sales probably increased by 30 to 40 per cent while population was practically stationary—perhaps moving by two or three per cent.[12] Raw cotton imports were rising similarly—by about 60 per cent for the period.[13] There were virtually no exports of domesti-

[10] Phyllis Deane, 1957, using wool consumed as a rough index of output in real terms.

[11] I have calculated value of output at constant prices using Deane's value figure for 1695 as a base. Exports at constant prices (Deane and Cole, *op. cit.*, p. 59) are deducted to estimate home consumption. 1695 is preferred as a base because her 1741 value of output is very low, perhaps because wool prices were abnormally low; to use it as a base creates distortions, e.g. it implies that 60–70 per cent of output was exported. Deane suggests 40 per cent in 1695. The calculation suggests an increase of about 39 per cent in home consumption between 1695 and 1741.

[12] See B. R. Mitchell and Phyllis Deane, 1962, Ch. 1, Table 1.

[13] Phyllis Deane and W. A. Cole, 1962, p. 51.

cally-produced cottons and imports of finished cottons were almost constant. With population stagnant, it seems that consumption of wool and cotton textiles per capita was rising substantially. Other indicators of industrial growth also show substantial increases. Indeed, of the indicators selected by Deane and Cole, only strong-beer production does not rise more rapidly than population between 1695–1704 and 1735–44.[14]

Deane and Cole argue that the falling food prices of this early period had little effect on industrial demand. They claim that the rising real incomes of non-farmers would not have brought expansion of industrial demand unless non-farmers' marginal propensities to consume manufactures were *higher* than farmers'[15]—whose real incomes would be falling. They appear to have disregarded the rise in national income which *ceteris paribus* should result from abundant harvests. The non-farmers would be the chief beneficiaries of both a redistribution of income as a result of differential price movements and the rise in total agricultural product. Their real incomes should have risen proportionally more than the fall in farmers' real incomes.[16] Therefore if non-farmers' marginal propensities were the same as farmers', or even if they were slightly less, there might be a rise in industrial demand when harvests were good, other things being equal. But Deane and Cole argue that other things were not equal.

In the first place the wage-earner's response to falling grain prices was to work less—thus presumably lowering money wages and offsetting, in part at least, the rise in real incomes which would otherwise have resulted from falling food prices (the argument is not supported by Deane and Cole's wage statistics,[17] but these, as they note, take no account of 'variations in the regularity of employment or the number of hours worked').[18] In the second place, part of the increase in real wages was taken up by the consumption of gin. Therefore much of the potential increase in purchasing power was absorbed either by increased leisure or by gin.[19]

Yet in discussing economic progress in the middle of the century Deane and Cole put great emphasis on what Donald Whitehead[20] has called the 'increased effort' thesis: that population pressure and rising food prices caused people to work harder to maintain their

[14] *Ibid.*, pp. 51, 288.
[15] *Ibid.*, p. 92.
[16] For a full discussion of this point see D. Whitehead, 'The English Industrial Revolution as an Example of Growth' in R. M. Hartwell, 1970, pp. 16 f.
[17] Phyllis Deane and W. A. Cole, 1962, pp. 18–22.
[18] *Ibid.*, p. 22.
[19] *Ibid.*, p. 93.
[20] D. Whitehead, 1964.

standard of living. Together these points imply that workers simply returned to the productive effort which they applied to their jobs before food prices fell. This means that 'increased effort' could hardly be as important as Deane and Cole imply. Perhaps it is more reasonable to suppose that the period of low food prices *did* raise standards of living and that this continued for such a long period that people had become accustomed to the improvement by mid-century and wished to maintain themselves at this new standard. The second quarter of the eighteenth century has been called the 'golden age' of the English labourer[21] and there is strong evidence to support the idea of rising consumption early in the century.

It is also possible to support this view by analysing birth- and death-rate movements in the eighteenth century, though this depends on some assumptions rather at variance with those normally used. Here also we move into problems relevant to the question of whether population growth was exogenous, a question which has puzzled historians for many years. It is a many-sided debate which we will not explore completely; but it has certain aspects which are relevant to our problems.

It is normally assumed that what has to be explained is the fall in the death rate in the middle of the century. In the period when population begins its upward movement, the birth rate remains fairly stable and so can hardly be the dynamic element. T. H. Marshall[22] suggests that for the *continuation* of growth it may be important to explain why the birth rate failed to fall in response to the falling death rate—as it normally would, given limited resources. However, this analysis can only come into play some time after the fall in the death rate had begun. With G. S. L. Tucker[23] we may use it to explain why population growth continued upward after 1770 or 1780, and to argue that this marked a break in trend from traditional rates of growth. However, this still leaves the falling death rates as the explanation of the initial upsurge of population between 1740 and 1780. But what does this interpretation assume? It assumes among other things that birth rates and death rates were 'normal' immediately before the upsurge of population began in the 1740s. What evidence supports this assumption? With the limited information available it may be unjustified. It is just as plausible to argue that death rates were abnormally high in the 1720s and 1730s and that economic influence had *already* raised the birth rate. If, for example, there had been a period of economic prosperity for the lower classes in the late seventeenth or early eighteenth centuries, there would have been a tendency for the birth rate to rise, and it *was* rising in the

[21] E. L. Jones, 1965, p. 18.
[22] T. H. Marshall, 1929.
[23] G. S. L. Tucker, 1963.

first half of the eighteenth century.[24] This would normally cause population to rise, but if there was a chance upward movement in the death rate (through a smallpox epidemic[25] and the gin mania) the effect of the upturn of the birth rate would be delayed until this period of abnormally high death rate disappeared. In short, it is at least as plausible to argue, as Tucker does,[26] that the death rate was abnormally high in the 1720s and 1730s as it is to assume that it was normal, and it is also reasonable to hypothesize that economic circumstances had already pushed up the birth rate.[27]

If this argument were correct it is more important to explain why the death rate rose in the 1720s and 1730s than it is to explain why it fell in the 1740s and 1750s. Indeed, it is easy to find reasons why the death rate may have been abnormally high in the former two decades—in the smallpox epidemic and the gin mania. On the other hand, if the death rate was normal in the 1720s and 1730s it is more difficult to find good reasons why it should have fallen subsequently. True, Razzell[28] has claimed to be able to explain the whole of the falling death rate in terms of inoculation, but his claim is not supported by his own evidence, which suggests that the spread of inoculation could not have caused a significant fall in the death rate before the late 1760s. He writes that 'inoculation did not become really widespread until after the 1760s':[29] that is until the Suttonian method reduced the risk of death from inoculation. Thus he still leaves unexplained that vital gap from 1740 to the early 1760s.

The other aspect of this hypothesis is that the birth rate had already risen for economic reasons before population growth got under way (to refute this, of course, would not refute the hypothesis about the causes of the death-rate movement), and that it was only the delaying effects of a chance upward movement in the death rate which prevented it from bringing about an earlier upturn in population. Further investigation of this hypothesis would need to go back into the seventeenth century, and the information is not available at this time.

Nevertheless, it is possible to see some confirmation of this hypothesis in the Deane and Cole regional figures, which also strengthen the idea that there was regional economic advance well before 1745. These regional figures show a strong upward movement of the birth

[24] G. Talbot Griffith, 1926, shows a marked fall in the first decade but subsequently a rise until 1750.
[25] See G. S. L. Tucker, 1963, pp. 212 ff.
[26] *Ibid.*
[27] Deane and Cole refer to the labour shortage of the late seventeenth and early eighteenth centuries, p. 89.
[28] P. E. Razzell, 1965.
[29] *Ibid.*, p. 318.

rate in the North-West from the early part of the century.[30] Later in the century the rise in the birth rate is even more marked, but the upward movement is obviously firmly established quite early in the eighteenth century. Birth rates also show a less marked but nevertheless pronounced upturn after the first decade in the South and the North.

This demographic picture is consistent with the hypothesis of economic advance in the North-west early in the century as demand for its cheap 'mass' products grew, and of the gradual involvement of other parts of Britain. The demographic picture is drawn from Deane and Cole; but the inferences we have drawn are at variance with their views about the growth of the home market for industrial goods in the first half-century. The inferences conflict with their views both that little industrial growth occurred in the first half-century and that growth in the home market for manufactures depended on farmers' prosperity. On their own evidence the population of 'industrial' counties was expanding at the very time when 'land tax and the competition of larger and more efficient estates drove some of the lesser gentry and yeomen to abandon the land for other pursuits' and 'landlords seem to have experienced difficulty in finding tenants'.[31] If demand from the farming community was the major element in home industrial demand, why did the industrial areas—and particularly the new industrial areas—expand so rapidly in such difficult times? Perhaps it could be argued that most of the expansion was an expansion of the export market rather than home market, but that may simply remove the problem of explanation one further stage, since imports rose more than exports between 1715 and 1740.[32] Who was demanding the increased quantity of imports at that time? How do we explain the growth of population in industrial counties and the general rise in the birth rate from the second decade of the eighteenth century? Perhaps it was the result of economic prosperity in the non-farming community which lifted constraints upon the birth rate: as M. W. Flinn writes, 'It is difficult to explain a significant rise in the birth rate in the pre-contraception era in other than economic terms.'[33]

It may be argued against this hypothesis that the observed upturn in the birth rate was simply a Marshall-type reaction to the rising death rate. More deaths increased economic opportunity, lowering the age of marriage or causing relaxation of family limitation within marriage: hence the birth rate rose in response to the rising death rate. It may be possible to entertain this idea except in the North-west, where

[30] Phyllis Deane and W. A. Cole, 1962, pp. 126–7.
[31] *Ibid.*, p. 96; see also p. 105.
[32] *Ibid.*, p. 48.
[33] M. W. Flinn, 1966b, p. 21.

the birth rate was already rising in the first decade *before* the death rate began its upturn. For other areas it is also possible that the birth-rate movements coincided too closely with the death rate: we would expect a lag[34] though it is clearly impossible to say much about this in the absence of data before 1700.

The implications of this hypothesis go deeper than perhaps appears at first sight. The case for making population growth a prime stimulus to growth in the eighteenth century rests upon the assumption that it was independent of economic influence—at least for the first twenty or thirty years of its upward movement. Tucker is able to argue persuasively for a break in the trend of population growth from 1770 or 1780 which was related to economic growth.[35] However, as long as we concentrate on the falling death rate to explain the growth from 1740 to 1780, most historians would agree that it was independent of economic influence. Of course, the death rate can be influenced by economic circumstances but there is little chance of disentangling economic from other influences at this time. More important, there is little in the history of the 1750s and 1760s to suggest that economic influence could have played a significant part in the fall of the death rate. Indeed, food-price movements suggest that the supply of foodstuffs may have been less plentiful than earlier in the century.

For these reasons recent opinion has seen the fall in the death rate in mid-century as simply a chance fluctuation—the result of good weather or the absence of disease.[36] Naturally this has worried historians, because population growth is still firmly established as a major factor in the eighteenth-century British economy. If indeed population growth was a major stimulus and if it occurred independently and by chance in the early stages, does this mean that the industrial revolution was fortuitous?

If the hypothesis outlined above is correct, of course the question does not arise, because the stimulus to population growth came late in the seventeenth century or early in the eighteenth century through a rising and then consistently high birth rate. It is accepted that the birth rate is usually influenced by economic conditions in pre-industrial societies (of course short-run fluctuations may be caused by age distribution, but we know nothing about this for the early eighteenth century). The impetus to population growth began much earlier than the period we now look to, and the effects of this impetus were temporarily halted by a chance upturn of the death rate early in the eighteenth century.

Even if this hypothesis is rejected, we need not see the population

[34] See T. H. Marshall, 1929.
[35] G. S. L. Tucker, 1963.
[36] H. J. Habakkuk, 1958, p. 500.

grow th as the controlling influence in the eighteenth century. It has yet to be shown that the growth of population before the industrial revo lution was in any sense unique. After all, the period was only some fort y years and population growth was not startlingly rapid in that forty yea rs—indeed growth was not uniformly high throughout. There is nothing in the demographic history of that period which suggests that it set up forces strong enough to lead to an industrial revolution, though it may have stimulated some growth. Moreover, Marshall and Tucker argue that population growth is normally fluctuant in the pre-industrial societies. If the upturn of population had not come when it did it would probably have come some time later, perhaps then releasing the same consequences as it did in the second half of the eighteenth century. We would have to accept that the timing of population movements influenced the timing of economic development, but we need not conclude from this that the industrial revolution would not have occurred if the death rate had not chanced to fall from the 1740s. This is just another way of saying that the potential for growth was present and that the upturn of population helped to release this potential. However, even if the pattern of population fluctuations had been different the potential would still have been there, and the industrial revolution would still have occurred—though with different timing.

All this seems to play down the role of population growth; but we must still acknowledge that it must have been a very important part of the extension of demand (though by no means the only aspect of that extension) and of course that it was an essential aspect of the growth of an effective labour supply.[37]

THE PUZZLE OF POPULATION'S ROLE

We have looked at population growth as it influenced demand. We have tried to estimate whether demand movements coincided with population growth or whether there was actually an important upward movement in demand—or perhaps, more correctly, a change in the nature of demand—prior to the population upsurge of the mid-eighteenth century.

The general problem of the relationship between population growth and demand is intriguing. After all, we know well enough that population growth in itself cannot always stimulate the economy. China and India are sufficient illustrations that population growth may only alter the distribution of income and may not raise overall demand sufficiently.

We do not know enough to illuminate the conditions in which popula-

[37] J. D. Chambers, 1952–3; H. J. Habakkuk, 1963, p. 614; L. J. White, 1969.

tion growth helps or hinders economic growth. In most traditional societies population probably needs to grow as the economy grows, because of the limited capacity of the agricultural sector to release labour—partly as a result of an innate immobility, partly because productivity improvements are likely to be slow at first. Whether the demand aspect of population growth will stimulate the economy will depend upon demand distribution at the start, changes in demand distribution, and how the resulting demand requirements match the natural strengths of the economy. If, because of subsistence requirements, demand is too heavily concentrated into sectors which do not have growth potential (perhaps because of foreign competition or limits to productivity improvement) the growth of population will distort the economy. Where population grows too rapidly, the economy must be weighted heavily in favour of basic supplies—foodstuffs and clothing —which limits growth rates of new industries. Obviously the impact of population growth will depend upon its rate of growth and the demand situation *vis-à-vis* the natural economic growth potentials in the economy. Thus the further study of demand is important to our knowledge of why the British industrial revolution occurred. The gaps in our knowledge of aggregates and distributions amongst classes perhaps suggest that the most fruitful approach to the problem at this moment may be through a study of consumer expenditure patterns, if suitable data can be found.

ANOTHER APPROACH TO THE BRITISH POPULATION PROBLEM

Recently there has been a new way of looking at the relationship between population growth and the industrial revolution. H. J. Habakkuk[38] argues that we may have to explain why population did not grow more rapidly rather than why it grew at all. Obviously he has in mind the recent difficulties of countries such as India, where economic advance has been accompanied by a rapid increase in population which tends to wipe out the advantages of progress. Why did population not expand to fill the economic gap in Britain, as so frequently happens in pre-industrial societies?

Professor Habakkuk explains the limited response of British population to economic growth in terms of the difference in the social unit in Europe as compared with India. In Europe the social unit was the 'nuclear family': a separate household established upon marriage, the husband being immediately and solely responsible for the welfare of the household. Contrast this with the Indian 'extended family' unit

[38] H. J. Habbakuk, 1965a, pp. 125 f.

where newly-weds become part of a larger family which may cover several generations, and in which the obligation for material welfare is spread over a number of people in the unit. In Europe the male tended to defer marriage until he thought himself able to support his family. In India, without direct and immediate personal responsibility, the same limitations were not so powerful. The European system therefore tended to slow down the rate of growth of population. In India younger marriages, and possibly the higher incidence of marriage, produced high rates of population growth once medical improvements reduced the very high death rate. In India economic limits on marriage, and hence on the birth rate, were not as strong as in Britain.

Of course, while this could be an important reason for the difference in the experience of Britain compared with many Asian countries, it is still not sufficient explanation of why the industrial revolution came first to Britain. The nuclear family unit was common to most of Europe. More important, it is doubtful if this thesis is convincing for eighteenth-century Britain. The influence of the different family systems is on the birth rate. Habakkuk's analysis is satisfactory where the death rate was falling very rapidly and there was a difference in the downward response of the birth rate: where, in Britain, the birth rate would decline with the death rate, in India it would not. This pattern occurred in the nineteenth century, so it might explain demographic differences then, but this was *not* the pattern of the eighteenth century. In that century the British birth rate did not react downwards and may even have risen after the death rate fell.[39] If it is claimed, therefore, that an extended family system would have seen British population rise even more rapidly in the eighteenth century, this could only have been by causing an even greater rise in the birth rate. But if the birth rate would have risen more under an extended family system, this implies a greater response to growing economic opportunity than is found in a nuclear family system. This is the reverse of what we would expect.

Nevertheless, the general concept is interesting and more investigation is required to see whether there were social attitudes in Britain which put limits upon the age at marriage, incidence of marriage or the size of families, and hence upon the rate of growth of population in the eighteenth century.

FURTHER READING

On population changes:
DEANE, PHYLLIS and COLE, W. A.: *British Economic Growth 1688–1959* (especially Chs. 2 and 3).

[39] See especially J. T. Krause, 1958–9a.

FLINN, M. W.: *The Origins of the Industrial Revolution* (Ch. 2).

* HABAKKUK, H. J.: 'English Population in the Eighteenth Century'.
  * 'The Economic History of Modern Britain'.
  'Population Problems and European Economic Development in the Late Eighteenth and Nineteenth Centuries'.

* HELLEINER, K. F.: 'The Vital Revolution Reconsidered'.

KRAUSE, J. T.: 'Changes in English Fertility and Mortality 1781–1850'.
  'Some Implication of Recent Research in Historical Demography'.
  † 'Some Neglected Factors in the English Industrial Revolution.'
  'The Changing Adequacy of English Registration, 1690–1837' in D. V. Glass and D. E. C. Eversley (eds.): *Population in History: Essays in Historical Demography*.
  † 'English Population Movements between 1700 and 1850.,

†* MCKEOWN, T. and BROWN, R. G.: 'Medical Evidence Related to English Population Changes in the Eighteenth Century'.

* MARSHALL, T. H.: 'The Population Problem During the Industrial Revolution: A Note on the Present State of the Controversy'.

†* RAZZELL, P. E.: 'Population Change in Eighteenth-Century England: A Reinterpretation'.

TUCKER, G. S. L.: 'English Pre-Industrial Population Trends'.

† WRIGLEY, E. A.: 'Family Limitation in Pre-Industrial England'.

* Reprinted in D. V. Glass and D. E. C. Eversley (eds.): *Population in History: Essays in Historical Demography*. Edward Arnold, London, 1965 (see also editor's introduction).

† Reprinted in M. Drake (ed.): *Population and Industrialization*. Methuen, London, 1969 (see also editor's introduction).

On population and demand:

COATS, A. W.: 'Changing Attitudes to Labour in the Mid-Eighteenth Century'.

COLEMAN, D. C.: 'Labour in the English Economy of the Seventeenth Century'.

DEANE, PHYLLIS and COLE, W. A.: *British Economic Growth 1688–1959*.

EVERSLEY, D. E. C.: 'The Home Market and Economic Growth in England, 1750–80'.

FLINN, M. W.: *The Origins of the Industrial Revolution* (Ch. 4).
  'Agricultural Productivity and Economic Growth in England 1700–1760: A Comment'.

GILBOY, E. B.: 'Demand as a Factor in the Industrial Revolution'.

HABAKKUK, H. J.: *Population Growth and Economic Development since 1750*.

JOHN, A. H.: 'Agricultural Productivity and Economic Growth in England 1700–1760'.

'Aspects of English Economic Growth in the First Half of the Eighteenth Century.'

WHITEHEAD, D.: 'The English Industrial Revolution as an Example of Growth', in R. M. Hartwell (ed.): *The Industrial Revolution.*

5 Science and Technical Abilities

Some science historians have seen the history of science as the 'key to modern history'. Although many economic historians recognize it as an important factor in the industrial revolution, they have not succeeded in clarifying its exact role. It is usually mentioned as an environmental factor. Its exact relation to the economy is seldom specified, and then usually in terms of its contribution to industrial technology, though some have stressed its educational role.

It is surprising that despite its periodic revival in general literature it has not really been discussed or debated at any great length. A partial exception is the debate about whether industrial techniques were science-based in the eighteenth century: but this is a debate largely confused in purpose and methodology which does not adequately explore vital areas of the relationship between science and economic growth. On one side of this debate Gillespie[1] holds that science contributed very little directly to industrial technology in the eighteenth century. Gillespie's argument is based mainly upon French studies, and Schofield[2] believes that his ideas do not hold true for Britain. Bernal's view[3] of the British situation, however, is similar to Gillespie's. The Bernal–Gillespie versus Schofield disagreement is less important than it appears to be since, as Gillespie argues, the two sides are talking about different things. To some extent it is a semantic difference. Science means to Gillespie 'abstract understanding of nature', while Schofield seems to mean 'technical activity'. However, the difference is more than just one of terminology.

Schofield obviously believes that the role of science has been underrated and he sets out to redress the balance, to show indeed that it did contribute to eighteenth-century industrial technology. He uses his studies of the Lunar Society of Birmingham to demonstrate mutual interest and help between industrialists such as Matthew Boulton and Josiah Wedgwood and scientists like Joseph Priestley and Erasmus

[1] C. C. Gillespie, 1957.
[2] R. E. Schofield, 1957 and 1963.
[3] J. D. Bernal, 1954, pp. 345–74 and 419–45.

Darwin. This eminent group not only met for discussion, they helped each other in practical ways. The scientists investigated some of the technical problems of the industrialists. In return, they were supported in their purely scientific research by the industrialists who provided them with apparatus and rooms for laboratories.

While Schofield's researches are interesting, particularly in showing the wide range of problems associated with an industrial revolution, his main aim is apparently to show that scientists did collaborate with industrialists and that they did contribute to industrial technology in the eighteenth century. However, perhaps he is attacking a straw man: a thesis that scientists did not contribute to industrial technology in the eighteenth century would be too extreme for most serious historians. Certainly neither Gillespie nor Bernal say that scientists contributed nothing to technology in the eighteenth century, either in France or Britain. Bernal does say that developments central to the industrial revolution were not the product of the application of new scientific principles, but were developed by practical men whom he calls 'the artisan inventors'.[4] Now this can be interpreted either as a judgement of the significance of certain inventions, i.e. those central to the industrial revolution—in which case it must be refuted in like terms—or as a way of saying that theoretical science did not lead to important new industrial techniques as was to happen in the nineteenth and twentieth centuries; but it cannot be interpreted as saying that scientists contributed *nothing* to industrial techniques.

If it is a question of assessing the relative significance of artisan inventors as against scientists, Schofield may believe he is on firm ground because he is apparently concerned with the whole range of inventions and improvements, not just the spectacular few. The major inventions have probably been over-rated and the myriad of small improvements to machines and processes under-rated. Although individually the small unsung improvements were only marginally important, collectively they may have been enormously important to economic performance. Yet if this observation can be used to support Schofield's approach, it can also be used to show that his methods are inadequate. This is not just because his study is too limited to support a generalization, though that is true. The deficiency is more basic: a list is not an assessment. Moreover, the whole concept of assessment in these terms is all but impossible: because it is surely impossible to trace all improvements; because there is no way of telling whether a particular example, such as Schofield's Lunar Society, is representative: and because it would be difficult if not impossible to estimate the economic significance of particular inventions. In short, his method is

4 J. D. Bernal, 1954, p. 370.

only satisfactory as applied to the uninteresting question of whether scientists contributed *anything* to technology.

The second interpretation of Bernal's statement is that science in the eighteenth century did not lead to new industries or transform industries by its discoveries, as it was to do in the nineteenth and twentieth centuries. The transformation of the chemical industry, the massive electrical and electronic industries and, latterly, atomic power have been the outcome of purely scientific discoveries. The *independent* investigations of science led to these enormously important technological changes; they were not made in response to some industrial problem.

Bernal acknowledges that in the eighteenth century scientists investigated the problems of industry, but he describes science as the handmaiden of industry. Perhaps he means that the problems investigated were posed by the industrialists and, in the absence of independent scientific discoveries with industrial potential, the initiative for technical progress remained with the entrepreneur. This may not be true without exception, but broadly the generalization appears to be sound. Bernal, indeed, goes so far as to suggest that industry did more for science than science did for industry in the eighteenth century, by stimulating a new interest in science among the newly arisen bourgeoisie as they recognized its potential in solving production problems. It is interesting that the latter part of this idea is completely consistent with what Schofield sets out to show.

Even if this debate is unresolved, and indeed some lines of it are unsolvable, it is clear that science did not play such an important direct part in industrial technology as it was to play later. There is, however, a second way in which science is thought to have influenced economic growth, through its educational and intellectual qualities. As Bernal writes, 'Although . . . the Industrial Revolution owed little to science, the men who directed its progress were thoroughly imbued with the scientific spirit.'[5]

There are perhaps three aspects of this educational contribution. The first is simply that scientific knowledge was used by inventors to give effect to their ideas. Moderately sophisticated mechanical design involved some knowledge of mechanics and mathematics. It was from the scientist that the artisan inventor learned the necessary skills—artisans 'absorbing as much science as they could turn to use'.[6] The second educational contribution of science was the thorough analysis and elucidation of industrial processes. Gillespie[7] emphasizes that the

[5] *Ibid.*, p. 372.
[6] *Ibid.*, p. 425.
[7] C. C. Gillespie, 1957, pp. 404–7.

scientist's function was to explain existing industrial techniques so that the underlying reasons for them were understood. The artisans who understood the processes they used were more likely to improve upon them. Gillespie shows that many eighteenth-century scientists thought that this was the most important aspect of their relationship with technology. Gillespie writes that science was applied 'very widely' to industry in this sense. However, if it was applied widely its practical influence was apparently not strong, at least in France, for Gillespie admits that 'the metal industries were not at first much changed by the development of the science of metallurgy; they simply began to be understood',[8] and, although metallurgy was given more scientific attention than other industries, 'the metal trades proved the least resilient in recovering from the drastic technological set-backs dealt to French industry by the revolutionary disturbances.'[9]

The third is a less tangible but perhaps more important educational function—teaching the intellectual processes by which the inventor solved a production problem. Perhaps the engineer learnt not only certain tools of analysis but the very form of analysis as well—a method of attacking his problem in a systematic way. As Gillespie writes of the experimental method, '. . . its mode of procedure is analytical. . . . it seeks to discern the essential elements of a complex subject, . . . it ranges and classifies them according to logical connections . . . [and] establishes systematic nomenclature'.[10] The new science involved a new intellectual approach which perhaps was passed on to the educated community, thus helping to train men's minds in orderly systematic analysis of a problem. James Watt said:

> Although Dr. Black's theory of latent heat did not *suggest* my improvements on the steam-engine, yet the knowledge upon various subjects which he was pleased to communicate to me, and the correct modes of reasoning, and of making experiments of which he set me the example, certainly conduced very much to facilitate the progress of my inventions.[11]

The influences which Watt acknowledges are obviously far more subtle and intangible than learning the accumulated mathematical and mechanical knowledge of the scientist. They may be even more important in explaining the triumphs of invention in Britain and Europe.

This idea is interesting because the literature undoubtedly contains an implication that industrialized peoples show intellectual qualities which are quite distinct from other cultures. This is sometimes stated as a superiority in abstract thought. It does not imply, of course, any

[8] C. C. Gillespie, 1957, p. 405.
[9] *Ibid.*, p. 400.
[10] *Ibid.*, p. 405.
[11] D. Fleming, 1952, p. 5.

inherent superiority—it is undoubtedly connected with intellectual environment and training;[12] but what is the nature of this environment and training, and can it be connected firmly with the scientific revolution?

There is, of course, a *prima facie* case for such a connection because of the broad coincidence of the scientific revolution and industrialization in Western societies. This does not necessarily mean that the scientific revolution led to the industrial revolution, since the scientific revolution from its origins was European in character and the industrial revolution was initially confined to Britain. Nevertheless, this does not rule out the possibility of the scientific revolution providing an essential intellectual training for solving a wide range of problems which first became pressing in the British economy. We are here concerned primarily with the underlying ability to solve problems, not so much with the pressures and motives for solving them, though the two are interconnected. It seems to be more than a coincidence that Japan, the only non-European society which has carried through industrialization, adopted a deliberate policy of borrowing from the European intellectual tradition. Other industrialized countries are either European or are offshoots of European civilization.

Nevertheless, the case cannot rest on this alone. Some other particular characteristic of European civilization may have been responsible for this broad association—perhaps Christianity, which has been described by some scholars as a materialistic religion.

We obviously need to go much deeper into this relationship, not only to establish it but also in order that we may trace the history of its development. We need to be more precise about the intellectual qualities of the new science, the qualities it conferred upon the community in general, and the nature of the interactions between it and society.

The initial problem is the layman's difficulty in understanding precisely what the scientific revolution was. Crombie's definition refers to '. . . two essential aspects, the experimental and the mathematical'.[13] The apparent simplicity of this definition is belied by two complications. First, it is clear that neither experiment nor mathematics was new to science in the seventeenth century. Robert Grosseteste, for example, was said to be using the experimental method and mathematics at Oxford in the early thirteenth century,[14] H. Butterfield says:

. . . over fifty years ago, the origins of modern development in science were being pushed back, behind Leonardo de Vinci, to the later Middle Ages.

[12] E. Hagen, 1962a.
[13] A. C. Crombie, 1952, p. 277.
[14] *Ibid.*, pp. 219 f.

. . . . George Sarton draws our attention to still earlier dates which mark the emergence in Europe of algebra, alchemy, and other studies under the influence of the Arabs.[15]

The distinction between earlier uses of the method and the scientific revolution proper must be based upon the generality of the experimental method. These techniques may have been known and practised before, but only by a tiny minority who appear to have had little general influence upon method. What *was* new in the scientific revolution was that the method of the few became the method of the majority; for the first time it pervaded the scientific world and became the norm by which knowledge was extended.

If this argument is acceptable in theory there remain great practical problems, because the second difficulty of the layman is to understand exactly what is meant by 'the experimental method'. The difficulty is that experiment and observation were not entirely absent from the work of the old natural philosophers any more than they were absent from Chinese science before 1500.[16]

It has been said that the new science used experiment systematically[17] but it is not entirely clear what this means in this context. The word 'systematic' means 'according to a plan', but it cannot be said that the observations and experiments of the natural philosophers were without planning (if indeed any experiment can be unplanned). Certainly the experiments of the seventeenth century were more complex than earlier, but this is a difference of degree not kind. The growing range of possibilities occurring to the experimenter is probably associated with the accumulation of knowledge, which results in the experimenter recognizing a wider range of possible influences upon natural phenomena. But a similar distinction is necessary between seventeenth-century and twentieth-century experiments, so this is not the distinction we seek. It appears that the distinction is to be found, not in the nature of the experiment itself, but in the part played by the experiment in the intellectual approach to a problem.

The old method associated with the name of Aristotle emphasized logic and argument. This was not without reference to the real world, because it was on the basis of observed natural phenoma that the natural philosophers proceeded; but their observations were limited and used principally as a starting-point. Once the starting-point was established the only limitation which the observations imposed was that the explanation should be logically consistent with them. But of course there were

[15] H. Butterfield, 1959, p. 343.
[16] A. C. Crombie, 1952, p. 218; J. Needham, 1964.
[17] A. C. Crombie, 1952, p. 274.

often alternative explanations which could be logically consistent with the original observations, and it is in deciding between the alternatives that the approaches of Newton and Aristotle differed. In the Aristotelian method the reliance upon logic and argument tended to bog down in endless debates about propositions and semantics. By contrast, the new science tried to choose between the propositions on the basis of *further* factual evidence; and this factual evidence was gathered through experiment—experiment designed to establish which of the possible explanations were consistent or inconsistent with the facts. Since in this approach 'facts' must be comparable, there is an emphasis upon measurement—hence the importance of mathematics in modern science.

The emphasis on deciding between possible alternatives only on the basis of factual evidence not only involved a change in the intellectual structure of the scientific approach but led inevitably to a change in the *kind of question* which the scientist would tackle. The Aristotelian was prepared to explain the whole universe and everything in it on the basis of his reasoning. What he did not know he was prepared to deduce by logic. The modern scientist, on the other hand, was not prepared to pursue a problem beyond the limits of his ability to apply facts to the task of distinguishing between alternatives. Consequently he became confined to that part of the world which he thought was verifiable, and came to concentrate upon proximate causes rather than first causes—hence his concentration upon solvable and verifiable problems rather than upon metaphysics.

What did all this mean to the 'artisan inventor'? What intellectual qualities did this encourage amongst non-scientists? First, the scientists taught a method of analysis: how a complex problem could be broken into elements and the properties of the elements investigated objectively and systematically, with the aid of experiment and mathematics. It taught, therefore, methods of simplification and analysis. Second, the new emphasis on the solvable and verifiable rather than the purely speculative problem was important—both because it demonstrated that science could be useful practically and because, by example, it increased man's confidence in his ability to solve problems. Science both demonstrated a growing ability to solve problems, and provided new methods by which problems could be tackled.

This implies that some aspects of the scientific revolution penetrated beyond the intellectual elite. Recent work tends to confirm that this certainly happened to the artisan inventors.[18] However, the penetration is mainly seen as an absorption of the analytical tools and knowledge of the scientists—the mathematics and mechanics—and even this is not approached systematically; above all, there is no detailed consideration

[18] A. E. Musson and E. Robinson, 1960–61 and 1969.

of the wider issue of the penetration of forms of thought and analysis. Moreover, if there is a supposition that there was penetration to the middle ranks, might this not also be true of the lower ranks? How far down the social scale did the new modes of thought penetrate? Where economic literature refers to the habits of thought of industrial societies, it implies that the special characteristics of 'Western' thought are apparent at all levels.[19] Perhaps it *is* necessary to alter the intellectual habits of the lower classes—in order that they may work effectively with more and more sophisticated machinery; or as the infrastructure of the economy becomes more important; or simply because a viable industrial society may need mobility between economic classes, and it is necessary to remove impenetrable educational barriers to ensure this mobility.

It seems from this discussion that there is a whole range of important and fascinating topics which economic historians have hardly touched upon. Does an industrialized country acquire special intellectual qualities throughout the social range (which is not to imply that all classes show the same intellectual qualities, only that intellectual differences between two cultures are apparent at all levels)? If so, how do we define these intellectual qualities; when and how were they acquired, and what was their economic influence? Are they related to the scientific revolution, and if so what was the nature of this relationship? Precisely what *aspects* of the revolution in thought penetrated various social levels and when did this penetration take place?

At first sight it seems highly improbable that any changes in the thinking habits of the lower classes were associated with the scientific revolution. The formal education of the lower classes came mainly in the nineteenth century, more than two centuries after the scientific revolution. There had been some worker education in the eighteenth century; even this is remote in time from the scientific revolution of the seventeenth century, but they may still have been interlocked. The underlying intellectual structure of nineteenth-century education must have been shaped by middle and upper-class habits of thought which had already been influenced by the scientific revolution.[20] We may also see the scientific and educational changes as two parts of a process of intellectual adjustment to a changing society. A growing economy throws up production problems which can be solved initially by new organizational forms and better techniques—the emphasis being therefore upon leadership. As the transition continues there emerge additional problems—problems of living in an increasingly complicated world, and of building and maintaining a technically complex capital stock which becomes more and more pervasive as the economy is

---

[19] E. Hagen, 1962a, pp. 17–19.
[20] A. C. Crombie, 1960, p. 13.

transformed. By that time leadership is no longer enough for growth to continue. Thus the main impulse for scientific and educational change may have a common source—the changing needs of a society in transition.

What is the evidence that the scientific revolution can be explained in terms of changing social needs? Certainly the scientific revolution is difficult to explain in other terms. For instance, it can hardly have been a simple matter of the evolution of scientific thought in which knowledge gradually accumulated and finally, by a sort of compound interest, developed to a point where the extension of knowledge was more rapid than ever before. In this view the scientific revolution would be the simple outcome of the earlier patient spade-work, but there is obviously much more involved, because Chinese science was probably much superior in the Middle Ages[21] and *it* did not follow a similar path. The chronological lead of the Chinese should have brought the scientific revolution to China in the first place, if it were only a matter of evolution, but it did not. Moreover, although Chinese science had been superior, it actually failed to absorb the new science despite increasing Western contact. Earlier still the Greeks and Arabs had brilliant intellectual achievements at a time when Western Europe was barbarous and intellectually backward.

Nor is the 'heroic explanation' any more convincing. If it had been the simple product of a few men of genius who happened to be Westerners, we would expect that their knowledge and teaching would also be taken up in the East after a time. However, there was quite a different response to the teachings of the men of genius in the two societies, and it is probably this response which is at the heart of the matter.

Historically the thesis of interaction might be as follows: European society increasingly faced a new range of technical problems from the Renaissance on. These technical problems were mainly associated with long distance navigation arising from geographic discoveries and with the commercial exploitation of these discoveries. They were not, of course, problems which concerned most men but only the social leaders or what might be termed the 'dynamic fringe'. The problems they faced were scientific problems, and this brought a new social significance to science. Not only was the type of scientific problem altered, but science came to a new and practical relationship with the community, which in turn stimulated interest in it. The great advances in science derived from these new relationships. It is no coincidence that the great scientific probings of the sixteenth and seventeenth centuries were connected directly or indirectly with navigational problems—estimating longitude

[21] J. Needham, 1964, p. 385.

was the major problem which might be solved either through astronomy (by establishing the relative position of the stars), or through mechanics (by building a truly accurate moveable time-piece—the chronometer). The empirical problems of navigation were properly tackled by the empirical experimental method, thus bringing a new relationship between science and the community.

One puzzle is how we may reconcile the idea that the scientific revolution was a response to social needs with traditional treatments which are invariably written in terms of the great men, Galileo, Newton, Lavoisier, Priestley and so on. But they are not irreconcilable so long as we do not try to argue that the great men had *no* influence, and so long as we take them as in some sense representative of their age. The great men, of course, inspired others to follow—if only to follow their methods and modes of thinking. However, their inspiration was influential mainly because of the environment in which it occurred. After all, there had been great men in the past, indeed men who had practised the experimental method, but they had been ignored and even pilloried by their contemporaries, and they had not inspired others to follow because their work had only limited relevance to the society in which they lived. The majority of scientists were conditioned by what they saw as the needs of their society.

Thus Newton was important because he led men's minds, but he led them not only because he was a genius but because his methods were appropriate to the problems of his age. He was a leader therefore by consent, not by intellectual force of arms. He represented in a sense the intellectual ambitions of his age, as well as contributing enormously to the fulfilment of these ambitions by clarifying and extending the ways in which they could be pursued. We must keep firmly in mind our own definition of the scientific revolution as the generalization of principles already known and practised for generations.

This thesis helps to explain some important problems—why Chinese science followed such a different course, and why the revolution within European thought took different lines in different countries. In contrast to the growing commerce and 'materialism' in Europe, China is said[22] to have remained almost entirely agrarian in economy, and anti-mercantile in philosophy. The state still encouraged science, but only towards those ends which it saw as serving the needs of society. Science remained basically unchanged in China because the society was basically unchanging.

This thesis may also explain why Britain's science had special characteristics. French science had its geniuses as did British, Italian and German, but it was principally in Britain that science took a practical

[22] J. Needham, 1964, pp. 390 ff.

bent, and it was in Britain that science and scientists as a whole had their greatest social influence in the eighteenth century. Whilst the scientific revolution had common elements throughout Europe, it was where its methods could be most fruitful that it found its greatest strength.

However, even if we decide that there were no causal interactions of this type, the interplays between science and society were enormously important because the influence of scientific change still depended upon acceptance of its implications. The history of machine-breaking shows that the influence of technical advance was partly dependent upon the reactions of those whom it affected most closely. It is not only that machine-breaking has varied in intensity, it is also that community reaction to the machine-breaking has varied, presumably according to the social and economic situation. It is quite possible to think of the changing aspirations of the elite harbouring a scientific revolution in splendid isolation. If the middle and lower classes remain divorced from this movement, its economic influence may be slight—as in France before the revolution,[23] Germany and Russia. Today's economic planner must realize that the *implications* of scientific and technical advance must be acceptable to the community. Training an intellectual elite may be useless if its message is unheard or misunderstood. Scientists may be useful only to the extent that they *persuade* society to change. Logic, no matter how powerful, may not be sufficient to convince a society that its traditions must be swept aside with a massive brush. Intellectual influence and downward penetration of new modes of thought must occur, and there is no reason to suppose that this is automatic.

If it is presumed that the long-term progress of science *was* determined by the condition of society, is it possible to reconcile this with our earlier emphasis upon science as an important determinant of economic growth and hence society? If both hypotheses hold, what was the nature of the interconnections involved? Perhaps one was the dynamic element and the other passive. This of course is the kind of thinking I attacked in the first chapter. If we look upon it as a simple follow-the-leader problem we will be setting ourselves an impossible and misleading task—a chicken and egg problem. One did not give rise to the other in a simple cause-and-effect mechanism. Over a long period each fed upon the other—there was a mutual and continuing interaction in which each was essential to the other. The 'cause or effect' approach is like trying to show that the growth in air traffic led to the present state of the science of aerodynamics, or conversely that aerodynamics explains the growth of air traffic. The truth is that each depended upon the other. The problems of building better aeroplanes

[23] C. C. Gillespie, 1957, pp. 406–7.

to carry greater traffic led to progress in aerodynamics, which in turn allowed more advanced aeroplanes to be built, accelerating the growth of the market which raised new problems in aerodynamics . . . and so on. One simply cannot separate the progress of the science of aerodynamics from the prosaic business of building aeroplanes. If more and more planes were not being built there would be little incentive to improve the science, and if the science had not progressed the construction of aeroplanes with a wider range of applications would have been impossible. There is no simple way of looking at this relationship— the continuous progress of aircraft construction depended upon the continual progress of aerodynamics and vice versa. They were inseparable partners in the long-run growth of the air transport industry.

Similarly, it is a mistake to separate the progress of science from the progress of the community in which it occurred. For this reason it is an error to think of the scientific revolution as a once and for all breakthrough in the seventeenth century, from which point science soared dizzily to the heights of the twentieth century by self-propulsion. It was only possible for science to continue its progress because it continued to be relevant to the needs of a progressive society (and society only continued to progress because science continued to meet those needs). Where the new science was not relevant it did not survive, except perhaps amongst an intellectual elite—as in Italy, where the position of the elite was more akin to Grosseteste than to Newton.

In the two-way 'progressive' connection there could be stimulus from either direction. Technical problems led men like Henry the Navigator to subsidize scientific investigation. On the other hand, the demonstration of the strength of ideas might lead men to copy them and so influence the environment, as the German educational system was to do in the nineteenth century. As with ideology, the adoption of the science of others can give an independent impetus. However, in the long run the effects of these stimuli depend upon reactions to them: ideas have an important impulse only to the extent that the community accepts their implications and puts them into practice. And of course the search for answers to new technical problems will only bring progress if answers can be found; the continuation of the search thus depends on the capacity for technical invention. The continued progress of each is dependent upon a continuing mutual interaction.

In the light of this complex relationship, what methods can be used to analyse the role of science and education in economic development? I believe that for the moment we must be content to trace the comparative history of these developments. Schematically we may look for the penetration of new modes of thought into the elite (i.e. the scientific revolution proper); into the middle classes, which is the stage at which science and scientific modes of thought will be used by a comparatively large number of artisan inventors; and finally into the working class.

In Britain the history of this penetration can only be sketched in a very broad impressionistic way. There is considerable disagreement about the timing of the scientific revolution, but it was clearly associated with the seventeenth century well before the industrial revolution. Some set the beginning with Bacon, others with Galileo or Newton. The timing of the second phase appears on present evidence to coincide with the industrial revolution, if we take as an indication the spread of philosophical societies, scientific literature, itinerant scientific lecturers, etc.[24] The third phase was long and more nebulous. If it is associated with working-class education, it began in the late eighteenth century but was chiefly associated with the nineteenth century.

The neglect of this general field is strange, and especially so because it is perhaps the best illustration of how instructive a pragmatic approach may be. An industrializing country obviously has a problem of education which extends over the whole social range. Priorities must be set, since education is enormously expensive. The main difficulty is in deciding whom to educate, with what particular aims, and when this should be done. This means programming education to fit the changing needs of the community, setting a series of goals so that expensive education will not be wasted, as it has been in India for example, but at the same time ensuring that it keeps pace with the intellectual needs of the community. It seems plain that in order to do this we must show with some precision what the changing intellectual needs of the community are—in various phases of economic growth.

It is clear that, while historians have not ignored the economic importance of science, their studies are based more upon an intuitive awareness of its importance than on a careful analysis. Moreover, we have not clarified the historical phases of the relationship between science and the economy and how we may seek to establish its history. In short we are uncertain about the key issues in the topic. For this reason present studies only throw light on a limited range of questions.

The history of science in relation to the industrial revolution turns out to be no less than an intellectual history, related to social and economic changes over a period of more than two hundred years. It would be best perhaps to approach the whole question from this point of view—trying to define the intellectual qualities characterizing the various levels of British industrial society, seeking the evidence for a change in the habits of thought of the various classes and tracing these historically in relation to social and economic change. One thing is clear, however. We must clarify in our own minds what we are trying

[24] A. E. Musson and E. Robinson, 1960-1 and 1969.

to do before we can seriously consider the methodological problem of how to do it.

FURTHER READING

ANDERSON, C. A. and BOWMAN, M. J. (eds.): *Education and Economic Development*.

BERNAL, J. D: *Science in History*.

BUTTERFIELD, H: 'The History of Science and the Study of History'.

CLARK, G. N: *Science and Social Welfare in the Age of Newton*.

CROMBIE, A. C: *Augustine to Galileo. The History of Science A.D. 400–1650*.

   'Historians and the Scientific Revolution'.

FLEMING, D: 'Latent Heat and the Invention of the Watt Engine'.

GILFILLAN, S. C: 'Invention as a Factor in Economic History'.

GILLESPIE, C. C: 'The Natural History of Industry'.

HAGEN, E: 'A Framework for Analysing Economic and Political Change'.

HALL, A. R: *From Galileo to Newton 1630–1720*.

HANS, N. A: *New Trends in Education in the Eighteenth Century*.

HURST, J. S: 'Professor West on Early Nineteenth-century Education'.

MATHIAS, P: 'Who Unbound Prometheus? Science and Technological Change 1600–1800'.

MUSSON, A. E. and ROBINSON, E: *Science and Technology in the Industrial Revolution*.

NEEDHAM, J: 'Science and Society in East and West'.

   The Grand Titration: Science and Society in East and West.

SCHMOOKLER, J: 'Economic Sources of Inventive Activity'.

SCHOFIELD, R. E: 'The Industrial Orientation of Science in the Lunar Society of Birmingham'.

SINGER, C. S. *et al.* (eds.): *A History of Technology*.

WEST, E.G: 'Resource Allocation and Growth in Early Nineteenth-century British Education'.

   'The Interpretation of Early Nineteenth-century Education Statistics'.

6 Foreign Trade

In dismissing the idea that any one factor should be given pre-eminence in explaining the industrial revolution I relied upon general arguments and did not examine any particular topic in detail. It may be best to fill this gap by looking at foreign trade, because this is perhaps the most plausible of the genus—a view recently reaffirmed by the work of a number of eminent historians.[1] Furthermore, although I find their general conclusion unacceptable, some interesting and important ideas are contained in these works.

K. Berrill writes: '...the most vital circumstance for the first industrial revolution was the market condition in the trading area, and this was only slowly ripening before 1780.'[2] Berrill is quoted with approval by Habakkuk and Deane,[3] and Whitehead also holds similar views: '. . . the reasons for making the growth of exports a driving force in British expansion seem compelling.[4] This view is based mainly upon the rapid growth of trade in the eighteenth century, especially after 1780, and upon the crucial role of foreign markets and sources of raw material supply for particular industries. The most important of these was the cotton industry, which was entirely dependent upon foreign raw materials and overwhelmingly dependent on the expansion of foreign markets in the crucial period of growth after 1780. In the last two decades after that date something like three-quarters of the increase in cotton textile production was exported, and by the end of the Napoleonic Wars three-quarters of the *total* production was going overseas.[5] Woollen textile exports also expanded rapidly in the last three decades, but the industry's total consumption of raw materials grew less rapidly, indeed less rapidly than population,[6] implying growing dependence upon exports. Iron exports were less significant but still accounted for a third of increased sales between 1788 and 1806.

[1] K. Berrill, 1954–60, p. 358; H. J. Habakkuk and Phyllis Deane, 1963; R. Davis 1954–5 and 1962–3; D. Whitehead, 1964.
[2] K. Berrill, 1959–60, p. 358.
[3] H. J. Habakkuk and Phyllis Deane, 1963, p. 78.
[4] D. Whitehead, 1964, p. 74.
[5] See Phyllis Deane and W. A. Cole, 1962, p. 185.
[6] Phyllis Deane, 1957, p. 220.

There is no need to carry the evidence further, however, because it is beyond dispute that foreign trade was vitally important to certain industries. Perhaps no-one could seriously doubt that the expansion of foreign trade was indispensable to rapid economic growth in the eighteenth and early nineteenth centuries. Deane and Cole for example, write: 'There can, of course, be no doubt of the central importance of overseas trade in the expansion of the economy during this period',[7] and in estimating industrial output they use overseas trade figures as an index of the growth of 'export industries' which are weighted heavily in their index of real output.[8]

However, Deane and Cole dispute the inferences usually drawn by advocates of foreign trade hegemony. They question the idea that foreign trade was *the* most important circumstance, the driving force, or prime stimulus of British economic growth. They also disagree that the growth of foreign trade was autonomous, i.e. that its growth was determined by circumstances outside the British economy. The first view rests upon the second to the extent that foreign trade could hardly have been a prime stimulus if its growth was the result of British economic growth. Perhaps this is the reason why Deane and Cole concentrate their attack on the second point—the autonomy of foreign markets. They begin by pointing out that there was an almost closed-circuit interrelationship between Britain, the Americas and West Africa. Not only did Britain come to depend increasingly upon these areas for sales and supplies,[9] but *they* also depended heavily upon Britain as a market and supplier. The southern colonies of America and the West Indies depended directly on sales to Britain for their foreign exchange earnings. The northern colonies and West Africa were indirectly dependent because they earned foreign exchange by selling (food and slaves) to the southern colonies and the West Indies. This pattern of trade has long been known of course but, as Deane and Cole show, recent work has tended to ignore the implications. The implications of this mutual dependence is that it is possible for growth at either end to have stimulated expansion. It may be true that the independent growth of the Americas was the leading stimulus (either by increased purchases of Britain's products and/or increased supplies of its own exports) in which case the stimulation to the British economy would have caused a reciprocal growth. However, it is equally plausible to argue the opposite case—that the stimulus came initially from Britain (because of her increased requirements of food and raw materials and/or because she was placing an increased quantity of goods on the international market).

[7] Phyllis Deane and W. A. Cole, 1962, p. 83.
[8] *Ibid.*, p. 78.
[9] Elizabeth Schumpeter, 1960.

This would in turn give rise to a reciprocal growth in the Americas. Contrary to what we might expect from recent literature, the two explanations are equally possible in theory. Deane and Cole argue that the dynamics of the situation will be indicated by the way in which terms of trade move. The terms of trade would tend to move against the Americas if growth was initiated mainly from there: they would be forcing sales of their own products and/or demanding British products beyond existing production levels. Conversely, the terms of trade would tend to move against Britain if growth came mainly from Britain: she would be trying to push sales beyond the current demands of the market and/or requiring more imports than the Americas were geared to produce. Deane and Cole claim that, as the terms of trade were moving against Britain, it was British growth which stimulated expansion, and that the growth of foreign trade was therefore not exogenous to the British economy.

There are a number of criticisms which can be levelled at the Deane and Cole thesis. Whitehead points out that they use gross barter terms of trade which may or may not reflect movements in net barter terms of trade (for which data are not available). But his completely opposite conclusion must be equally suspect on the same grounds. Indeed, Whitehead does not detail the basis of his contrary conclusion that '. . . in the crucial second half of the century the terms of trade probably improved'.[10]

Again, Habakkuk and Deane argue that British naval strength was the prime determinant of foreign trade expansion, not the British economic situation. If that were true the movements in terms of trade may not have had the significance imputed by Deane and Cole. However, Habakkuk and Deane's thesis is suspect. They argue that: 'The timing of the upsurge that appears in the overseas trade figures, however, seems to owe more to the fortunes of war than to technological change.'[11] They write that the cessation of fighting after the War of Independence would itself explain a large part of the upsurge. In part this upsurge was more apparent than real, because the tariff reform of 1784 probably sharply reduced smuggling and increased recorded imports.[12] In any case the short-run timing of trade fluctuations does not necessarily reflect the main factors underlying long-run trends. They make a stronger point when they argue that the French Wars of the 1790s crippled Britain's mercantile competitors on the Continent, opening substantial new markets for her. They point out that the volume of exports to Europe almost doubled in a decade, after a considerable

[10] D. Whitehead, 1964, p. 74.
[11] H. J. Habakkuk and Phyllis Deane, 1963, p. 78.
[12] W. A. Cole, 1957–8.

period of stagnation. They conclude from this that the expansion was at least as much the result of naval strength as of the efficiency of British manufacture. In European trade this may be so, but it is less important than it appears, because much of the expansion of exports to Europe consisted of re-exports as opposed to domestic exports. This growth must have had limited influence on the British economy, its influence being mainly on mercantile profits. It was certainly less significant than the growth of domestic exports, which were going increasingly outside Europe.

Nevertheless, even in trade to the Americas and Far East the point may still hold: there is no question that British naval power was an important trade advantage in time of war. Her strength was an advantage even in peace, enabling her to enforce the Navigation Acts, for example. But one may doubt whether this was of central importance. At least I do not think it is possible to support the inference that economic strength was secondary. The most obvious tendency in the expansion of domestic exports and retained imports was towards colonial and American sources, and Britain seems to have been supreme in these areas, quite apart from the fortunes of war. This is suggested, for example, in the rapid resurgence of trade with the U.S.A. almost immediately after Independence, despite the loss of political control and the enmities which the War of Independence created.

Moreover, a considerable part of the growth of the increasingly important cotton industry was at the expense of Indian cottons. British products replaced many grades of Indian textiles on the international market. It is difficult to believe that the exercise of British naval strength was decisive in bringing this about. There were, of course, established mercantile interests in this trade, and it would be strange if British naval strength were used against those interests. Of course political disturbances in India contributed, but this was mainly a short-run factor. The long-run explanation is the familiar story of British cottons being unable to compete freely with the Indian product until Arkwright's water-frame came into widespread use—after his patent was rescinded in the early 1780s. This and other economic improvements are probably the main reasons for the successful competition against Indian cottons.

Part of Habakkuk and Deane's argument is that improved economic efficiency could not have been important because the price of British cottons failed to fall in the period.[13] However, the relevant basis of judgement is the comparative price performance of British textiles—in a period when much of the trading world was affected by inflation as a result of the French Wars.

[13] H. J. Habakkuk and Phyllis Deane, 1963, p. 79.

Finally it must be admitted that even if Deane and Cole are correct, their argument is increasingly tenuous towards the end of the eighteenth century. Their analysis, based on movements in terms of trade, is plausible so long as the Americas derived nearly all of their foreign exchange by sales to Britain. But the analysis becomes less persuasive as the Americans increasingly tapped markets outside Britain. If the Americas could sell on foreign markets other than the British market their total foreign sales might expand even though their British sales did not. With an increasing command of foreign exchange they might then increase their purchase of British manufactures—thus exogenously stimulating the British economy. Consequently a leakage from a closed-circuit Atlantic system weakens the Deane and Cole analysis; and increasing American sales to Europe after Independence suggests that their analysis may be less and less persuasive from that time onwards.

On the question of autonomy, I suspect that Deane and Cole may be right for much of the eighteenth century—because the Americas were overwhelmingly dependent on the British market, because part of the growth was achieved by British products replacing Indian cottons, and because their evidence of terms of trade movements lends *some* support to the thesis. Nevertheless, the evidence is far from conclusive and a major study would be needed to resolve the issue.

While the debate about autonomy is intellectually stimulating, I would argue that for our purposes it may be a misleading and mistaken question to pursue. It seems to provoke an inevitable overemphasis of one side of the trading relationship. To illustrate the point, let us suppose that the growth *was* principally the result of autonomous pressures. This presumably means that economic growth within the Americas was greater then the demands for raw materials from British industry: thus American expansion was too rapid to 'balance' with British growth. Even if this were true, however, it is still impossible to explain the growth of trade without reference to the British economic situation. If American exports were growing too rapidly for British demands this could only continue over a long period if the British economy had the ability to make effective use of increased raw material supplies at falling prices, i.e. if the British had the capacity for continued expansion. Alternatively, if American demand for British goods caused the increase, how did they command the foreign exchange to make their demand effective—by borrowing (from Britain), or by selling more (to Britain)? In either case the growth of the market was only possible in the long run if the British economic situation was favourable—either because British exports in excess of imports could be financed, or because the British were capable of balancing greater demands from the Americas by absorbing the imports offered by the Americas. Moreover, the eighteenth century was not the first occasion on which there had been an expanding market to exploit; and the explanation of what happened must show why Britain was able to command this particular market expansion so effectively. For this we must look to Britain's economic, political, and naval strengths to see why she captured such a disproportionate share of the market. The main point is that the growth of this trade cannot be explained simply in terms of the independent growth of the Americas (if that is what happened): it must also be explained by many aspects of the British situation. After all, it is hardly feasible that the settlement of the Americas would have proceeded so far without an appropriate expansion of the market. The settlement must have been controlled to some degree by market capacities—unless men were prepared to go into the wilderness expecting to live self-sufficiently. Men would hardly move into new lands unless they expected to be able to sell their products, and the process of settlement could hardly have been continued for long unless these expectations were being satisfied. It is obviously foolish to ignore the development of British markets in explaining the extent of economic development in the Americas. they pushed to wait for pull.

Alternatively, if after our major study we decide that the growth of trade was indigenous to the British economy, this does not allow us to ignore conditions in the trading area. There is nothing inherently remarkable about a situation where the British economy was expanding and seeking new markets and new sources of supply—the Dutch had done the same thing before them. Where the British situation was unique was the nature of the interconnections which followed, in that the Americas expanded so rapidly, were tied so effectively to Britain, and fitted her needs so well both as a supplier and a market. In other words, the expansion achieved was only feasible so long as the Americas could match the British expansion. The fact that they did so, in the way that they did, was not simply the result of the British economic situation.

Therefore we do not explain the part played by foreign trade, nor why it was able to expand at the rate it did by establishing that it was or was not autonomous. Indeed, one may argue that trying to establish this is misleading, because it tends to concentrate attention on one side or the other. The truth is that we can only explain why trade grew as it did by looking at both sides of the trade. It was expanding both because of the British economic performance and because of the unique nature of the American market. This is obvious enough, but we are in danger of losing sight of the point, and distortions *have* occurred by doing so. This is illustrated by part of Habakkuk and Deane's argument. In trying to establish the primacy of foreign trade they argue that it is not acceptable to look to the new industries to explain acceleration because 'the industries which responded to innovation were a mere fraction of the national total at this stage'.[14] But they argue that the foreign trade growth was sufficiently sudden to suggest a breakthrough, and that this sector was capable of having important multiplier effects. However, the two classic innovating industries, cotton and iron, were the very ones which were the leaders in this breakthrough of foreign trade. Between 1772–3 and 1797–8 exports of these two industries accounted for forty per cent of the increase in domestic exports and by the end of the following decade their importance is even more marked—they account for well over half the increase in the previous thirty years. The point is of course that, if exports were the driving force, then the export industries were the essential medium through which this drive was exerted. They seem to be the very industries which Habakkuk and Deane dismiss as being relatively insignificant.

From another point if view, what would be the policy implications of emphasizing autonomy or non-autonomy? If growth were autonomous should the developing country seek to solve all its problems by finding a rapidly expanding market? But this will not serve if it cannot exploit the market. Equally, if non-autonomy is the answer, should it assume that internal expansion will automatically be reflected in expanding external markets? This is even more obvious nonsense in a world of protected and limited markets. For a country such as Britain, which must complement her resources and markets externally, the answer is that only both will serve—capacity for internal growth and improvement *and* access to an external market capable of rapid growth. And so it was in the eighteenth century. This does not invalidate the discussion about autonomy, but it does suggest that it is less important than it appears at first sight. Deane and Cole are correct in asserting the two-way relationships in trade patterns, and their work can help to reject the main thesis of the 'driving force' school of thought. What is dangerous in their arguments, however, is that they may cause us to switch from one unbalanced view to an opposite but equally unbalanced one. We must realize that, although the 'driving force' idea is unacceptable, important points are made by its advocates.

As Berrill says, the slow ripening of the American market was an important factor in the growth of trade (though it was not *the* most important factor). British naval strength also played a part (but Habakkuk and Deane take the argument too far). The growth of foreign trade is really only explicable in terms of *all* these things and others as well.

The expansion of foreign trade therefore depended upon the condi-

[14] H. J. Habakkuk and Phyllis Deane, 1963, p. 77.

tions at both ends of that trade, and we must explain what these conditions were if we want to show how and why it was able to expand as it did. At the British end it depended upon rapid economic growth—giving rise to greater demands for raw materials and foodstuffs and creating the ability to increase export production at competitive prices. The ability to increase exports depend upon a number of interconnected factors. Indeed, it may be thought that it must be explained in terms of all the elements which combine to give the British economy its particular character. For instance, the ability to support rapidly-growing export industries depended upon the ability of British agriculture to support a growing population which was increasingly non-agrarian (at least after 1780). Therefore the growth of foreign trade depended upon the ability of British agriculture to adapt itself to a new situation—involving fundamental changes in many farmers' habits and methods. More directly the growth of, say, cotton exports depended upon increasing efficiency in that industry, with all that that implies in terms of new levels of inventive ability, innovation, entrepreneurship, transport, capital organization and so on. In a very real sense the export performance of the British economy, and the growth of its demands, were the outcome of the history and character of the whole British economy.

Similarly, only a complex of important factors can explain the American aspect of this growth. For instance, political domination by Britain was probably a reason for Britain's monopoly of much of the trade. In the U.S.A., even the growth after Independence may be thought to depend on connections established during the period of British domination. In turn, the effectiveness of this domination was partly the result of British naval strength. The ability to make effective use of political domination depends to some extent upon the ability to enforce stated policies. As the Spanish and Portuguese discovered earlier, particularly in the West Indies, this principally depended on the sea power of the mother country.

Although political domination through the Navigation Acts was one reason why these areas leant heavily upon primary production and imported manufactures, it is easy to exaggerate the significance of these policies. 'Natural' causes also played their role. The advantage of the Americas was the abundance of land, which encouraged extensive methods of cultivation. The scattered market and the shortage of labour was a natural barrier to manufacture in competition with the British, whose large and compact domestic market and many trade connections offered greater opportunities for economies of scale in production. These factors, rather than the mother country's prohibitions, may have been the main determinants of the agricultural specialization of the Americas. Nevertheless, we may still suspect that Britain could not have achieved market penetration in a politically hostile community on a sufficiently large scale, and to this extent the political domination obviously played a part in the share of the market which Britain was able to command.

Perhaps more importantly, the rapid growth of the Americas depended upon the conditions there and the history of the area. Such rapid growth was only possible because over a long period the area had become a specialist agricultural economy, which was both capitalist and expansionist in outlook. These characteristics had been built mainly in the tobacco trade, but the area was also physically suited to cotton growing and consequently the switch in emphasis was comparatively easy and rapid. The extensive form of agriculture was only possible because the area had been sparsely populated by a people unfamiliar with modern weapons, and it could therefore be relatively easily colonized by Europeans. The Europeans who came were perhaps naturally adventurous and consequently more willing than their fellows at home to undertake the risks of catering for an expanding and changing market. This was of special significance because the bulk of British demands from overseas *was* for agricultural products and therefore required large areas of land producing commercially. By contrast, Japan's requirements in the twentieth century were mainly mineral, which required physical penetration of smaller areas and therefore perhaps involved fewer complications. The comparative abundance of land and the possibility of rapid settlement may have also been a factor in the very rapid growth of population in the Americas in the eighteenth century, which itself determined its growing trade capacity.

Finally, British domination of this trade may have been partly the result of other non-economic factors such as the experience gained by the British in long-distance trade during the seventeenth century.

It appears that the argument that the expansion of trade depended on the character of both British and American expansion refutes the hypothesis that foreign trade was a prime stimulus. If trade expansion depended upon conditions within Britain it is certain that some of these conditions had little to do with the growth and nature of foreign trade. We have argued, for example, that it depended upon the capacity of agriculture to fit into the pattern of economic change. Agriculture was only able to do this because of a long history of change, many aspects of which had little or no connection with foreign trade. It is difficult to see, for example, any significant connection between foreign trade and the change of parliamentary attitude to enclosure.

Yet perhaps this all means that there is after all a sense in which it is true that the market condition in the trading area was *the* most vital circumstance. There were many indispensables to the industrial revolution; the growth of foreign trade was one of these, and perhaps it was unique, and the most difficult of all to achieve. Perhaps it would have been possible to have developed the other indispensables in different ways or to have substituted alternatives serving the same purpose. It is certainly true that the growth of British foreign trade was built upon an extraordinary dominance in areas of trade which had extraordinary characteristics. The dominance and characteristics were established over a long period and perhaps partly fortuitously. Thus the geographic swing in world trade from Europe in the eighteenth century favoured Britain, because it was in the extra-European areas that Britain had gained control in the seventeenth century. She had also built up experience and institutions favourable to long-distance trades. This was perhaps largely fortuitous, since it was only because Britain had been unable to compete successfully with the Dutch in Europe that she had turned to the new areas. Similarly, the Navigation Acts which played a part in Britain's dominance in the eighteenth century had been passed in the seventeenth century, but were then principally directed against the Dutch in Europe. In this purpose they had been unsuccessful, perhaps even positively harmful,[15] but by good fortune they became an important peg in another trading sphere a century or so later.

In the light of these bases to British trade in the eighteenth century and of the importance of foreign trade to economic growth, is it not possible to argue that this was the most vital of the indispensables—the most difficult for Britain to do without? Perhaps, but one may wonder how such a view could be established, or even on what grounds it could be argued. How could it be shown that it was more difficult than agricultural reform, or the intellectual changes stemming from the scientific revolution, or the secularization of men's attitudes? The points made about the growth of trade arise from the history upon which the growth of the eighteenth century was built. Historically it is legitimate and indeed essential to emphasize these bases (but the same is true of the other indispensables we have mentioned). To emphasize this history does not involve a presumption that alternative developments were impossible. For instance, if Britain had not already controlled key areas, could she not have used her growing strength to extend control over them? She did in fact do so in India, Canada, the interior of what became the U.S.A. and in the Malay Peninsula, amongst others. Moreover, it is possible that the areas which Britain controlled at the beginning of the eighteenth century developed so quickly precisely because they were British. If she had controlled other areas—say in South America—perhaps they would have developed in the way that the northern continent did.

[15] G. N. Clark, 1925; V. Barbour, 1930.

In the end such debates are futile and sterile. The truth is that there were a number of indispensables and there is little point in trying to elevate one above the others in explaining economic development. We should be content to trace the development of each and to investigate the historical relationships involved as far as possible.

A great deal of useful work has been done on this topic, but we are in danger of dissipating this valuable knowledge by pursuing misleading and unbalanced questions. There are still legitimate questions of importance to be answered, such as that of the relative importance of British political strength and economic factors in explaining the development of the Americas, but our present methods are unsatisfactory for this purpose because they normally lead to emphasis of one factor to the exclusion of others. Another danger is the danger of 'infinite regression', because it is possible to argue plausibly that many factors contributed to the growth of British foreign trade. Topic 'introversion' (see Chapter I) leads towards that danger, a danger which will only be avoided if research is constantly pursued within a balanced framework. This balance must always be explicit, both in the method and in the conclusions.

FURTHER READING

BERRILL, K.: 'International Trade and the Rate of Economic Growth'.
CAIRNCROSS, A. K.: 'International Trade and Economic Development'.
* COLE, W. A.: 'Trends in Eighteenth-century Smuggling'.
* DAVIS, R.: 'English Foreign Trade 1660–1700'.
  * 'English Foreign Trade 1700–1774'.
DEANE, PHYLLIS and COLE, W. A.: *British Economic Growth 1688–1959*.
FARNIE, D. A.: 'The Commercial Empire of the Atlantic, 1607–1783'.
HABAKKUK, H. J. and DEANE, PHYLLIS: 'The Take-off in Britain'.
* JOHN, A. H.: 'Aspects of English Economic Growth in the First Half of the Eighteenth Century'.
RAMSAY, G. D.: *English Overseas Trade during the Centuries of Emergence*.
WHITEHEAD, D.: 'History to Scale? The British Economy in the Eighteenth Century'.

* Reprinted in Minchinton W. E. (ed.): *The Growth of English Overseas Trade in the Seventeenth and Eighteenth Centuries*.

7 Entrepreneurship and Capital Formation

The neglect of social influences upon economic performance is apparent in a number of important aspects of British studies. We have already touched upon some of these areas of neglect. Let us now turn to two other areas in which that neglect is also apparent: entrepreneurship and capital formation. Obviously both are important economic factors, and both have been the subject of intense theoretical and historical study. I do not propose to examine each of these comprehensively but only to make some observations relevant to one of my themes: the neglect of relationships between the economy and the kind of society in which economic factors operate.

MUTUAL INTERACTION BETWEEN THE ENTREPRENEUR AND SOCIETY

There is no doubt that shortage of entrepreneurs is one of the major unsolved problems of the aspirant developing country today. Nor is there much doubt that the supply of dynamic and able entrepreneurs is influenced by a number of factors such as the size of the market, growth of the market, and so on. I believe that amongst those factors the social environment in which potential entrepreneurs have been nurtured is amongst the most important. But how do we study this element?

The reasons why entrepreneurship differs from one country to another, and from one time to another, are highly complex. This complexity is reflected in divergent points of view on the role of entrepreneurship in economic development. These range from the view that entrepreneurship is a primary cause of economic development to the view that it is latent in any community, and that only opportunity is necessary to release the latent reservoir of talent. Perhaps both views have an element of truth. I mean by this that basic entrepreneurial talents are no doubt present in any large body of men, and that economic growth tends to draw out this talent; but it is obviously not an automatic or an easy process, as some economists imply, and this has important implications. Talent does not emerge easily and automatically, because the full potential of entrepreneurial talent is only realized in a favourable environment, and unfortunately the business environment in an under-developed country is generally far from favourable. The basic ethos is usually anti-entrepreneurial and severe social and legal barriers normally constrain the entrepreneur. This is not accidental: a society which is economically stagnant can only remain in harmony and stability if the *status quo* is basically unchanging. Those who rise rapidly to wealth are seen to do so at others' expense, and thus the ambitious are con-demned. In such a context this is a perfectly sound idea: if the national cake remains the same size he who increases the size of his slice does so at the expense of someone else. Richness itself is no threat if it is confined to those already rich, but the *nouveau riche* threatens the established order. Men who aspire to rise above their station are a deadly threat to the stability of life and the passivity of the masses, and hence a threat to social order and established authority.

It is no easy task to remove an ethos designed to preserve stability in a stagnant economy. Values and beliefs are difficult to alter at any time and especially so if they are part of the moral code, as the ideas which constrain business normally are. Men are inclined to regard moral attitudes as absolutes which are immutable, instead of being related to circumstances. Comparative studies both in time and space make it clear that moral attitudes are related to circumstances: but man clings to his old moral code even when circumstances are altering. And since the survival of the old moral code may inhibit some new forms of business, the growth potential of the economy is restricted, that is to say, a community's ethos and economic growth mutually interact on each other.

Mutual interaction might be explained as follows in the context of our problem. Ideas can limit economic growth by restricting a key economic element: the number of able entrepreneurs. If economic growth can be slowed by such a key element, then the pressure upon ideas about this key element is limited because growth is limited. Nevertheless, if growth continues for long enough ideas will gradually give way under the pressure of changing reality and by giving way will lift the restrictions on entrepreneurship and hence on economic growth. This implies of course a cumulative process, with the speed of economic growth and the speed of changing ideas about entrepreneurs influencing each other in a continuous and mutual interaction. It is the mutual interaction which makes the entrepreneurial problem so difficult to analyse.

This problem is complex in another sense also, in that the environ-ment in which the entrepreneur works is made up of a number of factors which can influence his abilities and the methods he can use, as well as the number of men who may aspire to be entrepreneurs. Thus the community, by defining achievement, can influence the internal goals of those who become businessmen. It can be defined as accumulating personal wealth, raising the status of a kinship or clan group, building something worth building, providing employment for more and more people, accumulating political power and so on. Society can also determine entrepreneurial capacities through the education that entrepreneurs are offered, both formally and informally.

Society can also define constraints within which most entrepreneurs will work. Some of these will be legal constraints which directly influence the methods entrepreneurs can use—the terms on which they can employ people, the terms on which they can borrow money, etc. Other constraints will be purely social. Some social constraints bear directly upon the entrepreneur, and he will respond if he is socially conscious. These include the psychological pressures which can be brought to bear if, for instance, he introduces a new machine allowing him callously to dismiss large numbers of employees. Other aspects of the social environment will influence him whether he is socially conscious or not, because they affect the commercial risk which he faces. Thus the political climate and political stability may increase or decrease risk. The legal system may be favourable or unfavourable to business according to its ability and willingness to enforce contracts, protect property, and so on.

The most vital question to my mind is not whether social influences upon entrepreneurship are important: they obviously are. The vital question is how we may study these influences in a way that will be instructive. I believe that the quality of entrepreneurship clearly influences economic performance, and an explanation of variation in entrepreneurial quality and vigour is a vital problem for underdeveloped countries struggling to remedy entrepreneurial deficiencies. (Indeed, if some scholars are correct in their diagnosis of the British economic malaise of the late nineteenth and twentieth centuries, it is not only a problem for underdeveloped countries.)

I will say immediately that I see no prospect of a direct and completely satisfying approach to this problem at this stage—it is beyond our competence. A direct approach would involve such questions as: to what extent did shortage of entrepreneurs inhibit economic growth in the seventeenth century? How far was this shortage the consequence of anti-entrepreneurial attitudes? How much more quickly would the economy have grown if the Tudors had not tried to restrict enclosure? I fear that we must be content with less.

Nevertheless, I believe that historians may ask some interesting questions, the answers to which would greatly interest the modern underdeveloped country. First, what factors appear to have influenced the supply and creativeness of entrepreneurs in the past? This may be indicated by a comparative investigation of entrepreneurship, such as Hoselitz's study of French and British entrepreneurs in the eighteenth century.[1] Second, how long did it take to remove specific limitations on the supply and the creativeness of entrepreneurs? This can also be studied in historical context. Third, what has to be done to remove the limitations? This can be the subject of theorizing but it can also be the subject of historical investigation. In historical terms this amounts to a study of the circumstances in which changing entrepreneurial environments have occurred. The historian would thus be involved in a study of the evolution of a favourable entrepreneurial environment. To know something of what constitutes a favourable entrepreneurial environment is not enough; we also need to study the emergence of that environment.

I do not pretend that we will come to any general conclusion in these studies. The constraints under which Japanese entrepreneurs worked were different from those influencing the British, but we may be able to gain some useful insights into the process of entrepreneurial emergence.

The view that entrepreneurship tends to emerge as a result of the opportunities of economic growth certainly has some merit, but I believe it ignores the inhibitions imposed by the social factors outlined above. Indeed, it is probably true that economic growth *tends* to produce entrepreneurs, and that social factors determine the rate at which the emergence can take place. If so, the really important issues are dynamic —how quickly attitudes towards entrepreneurs will alter and what factors influence the pace of these changes.

SOCIAL INHIBITIONS TO ENTREPRENEURSHIP

There are of course those who state or imply that these things are no real problem anyway. Hirschman, for example, seems to think that enterpreneurs emerge naturally within the process of growth itself.[2] However, it is clear that, while there may be a tendency for growth to influence the number of suitable entrepreneurs, the timing of their emergence will not necessarily correspond with the speed of economic growth to produce a smooth interlocking. Hirschman is perfectly well aware of this, as we see from his discussion of social influences upon entrepreneurial behaviour.[3] Moreover, although he specifically mentions

[1] B. Hozelitz, 1955; see also D. Landes, 1949 and 1951.
[2] A. O. Hirschman, 1961, p. 3.

entrepreneurs as a factor latent within a society, he emphasizes the absence of 'genuine decision-making' as a missing factor in most under-developed societies, and many aspects of his 'genuine decision-making' seem to be entrepreneurial as I understand it.

Gerschenkron appears to argue that entrepreneurship is latent in any society, and points to landlords, moneylenders and merchants in underdeveloped societies to illustrate the point.[4] But we cannot assume that because there are some entrepreneurs that there are enough. The medieval merchant princes are not truly relevant to the problem of developing economies precisely because they were the exception not the rule. They were men who were the mavericks of the society they preyed upon: they held their position because they were willing to go against the *mores* of their society. Their own peer group may have accepted their actions, but most men regarded them with hatred or suspicion. Our concern is to establish the conditions of a thoroughly commercialized and integrated economy. It may be possible for a sub-stantial and important merchant class to be established in the face of general community disapproval, but if the full range of economic activities is to be adequately supplied with dynamic entrepreneurial skill it is almost certainly necessary for the value system to tolerate and even acclaim entrepreneurial activities. Also, in the long run it is not desirable that entrepreneurs should be drawn exclusively from one social class—and it is perhaps *necessary* that they are not. This is partly so that a range of new talent is continually available, but also so that class interests and prejudices do not proscribe some kinds of enter-prise.

Of course a group which is already socially outcast for other reasons (e.g. the Quakers in England) may be the first to break through the barrier of social disapproval, but such groups do not exist in all societies. In any case this group may not be large enough. The principal point is that in an industrial community entrepreneurship needs to be widely based. Although a minority of the population will become entrepreneurs, it is still a substantial minority if we include industrialists, commercial agricultural producers, merchants, providers of transport, etc. It is therefore probably essential that entrepreneurs should be socially accepted in an industrial community.

BRITISH ENTREPRENEURSHIP

I will now turn to a short consideration of the present state of knowledge

[3] A. O. Hirschman, 1961, pp. 11–24.
[4] A. Gerschenkron, 1953.

of entrepreneurial problems in British growth. There is interesting historical work which suggests that eighteenth-century British entrepreneurs were bolder innovators than their Continental counterparts. It appears that Britain was not only prolific in invention, as every schoolboy knows; she also more readily put invention to practical use. This had two aspects. First, there seemed to be more entrepreneurs willing to undertake the hazards of bringing a new technique up to commercial standards and to actually apply it in business. Thus we find new processes being taken up in Britain, and even cases of Continental inventors bringing their processes to Britain after unsuccessful efforts to solicit local business interest. Frederick Konig brought his steam printing press to Britain, where the London *Times* made the first use of it in 1814. Subsequently Konig returned to Germany and raised local finance to make the machine which had previously interested no one.[5] Moreover, once the commercial possibilities had been demonstrated British businessmen as a whole seemed more willing and even more anxious to use recent techniques than their Continental counterparts. Thus most of the cotton textile machines developed by the British had been brought to France and actually used in businesses within ten or twelve years of their application in Britain.[6] However, French businessmen ignored the new machines on the whole, despite the example of both British and home producers. By contrast the British businessmen turned eagerly to the new machines, despite institutional blockages in their paths. Many of the early innovators had to fight to keep their patents intact against the encroachments of their competitors.

In explaining this difference it is easy to turn to the difference in commercial possibility—the ready access to a rapidly growing market for the products of British industry. And there is no doubt that this explanation is partly correct. Yet from a long-term view it is not sufficient to put all emphasis upon economic opportunity, because innovation also depends upon *responsiveness* to economic opportunity. It is clear that responsiveness is not simply and positively correlated with opportunity. This is shown by the differential responses of different well-defined groups in some communities. The Jews in many parts of Europe, the Chinese in South-east Asia, the Indians in Fiji, for example, reacted to opportunities more readily than others in those same communities. Indeed, since these groups were often persecuted minorities they probably had less opportunity than the majority. Their responses were different perhaps because their motivations were different, or they worked under different mental or social constraints, but not because they enjoyed greater economic opportunity.

[5] W. O. Henderson, 1965, p. 161.
[6] *Ibid.*, Ch. 2.

We have a sprinkling of important work which tries to show the ways in which the British economy was favoured by more dynamic entrepreneurship. But little has been done to investigate the basis of this superiority—to trace its evolution and the circumstances surrounding its evolution. We are far from being able to specify the exact reasons for the dynamism of the British. *Why* did the British entrepreneur fight to break patent protection, while the French disdained freely offered technical improvements?

Many recent studies of British entrepreneurs are not particularly helpful in answering such questions. Most are written about the great figures of the industrial revolution. Little has been done to investigate the host of lesser figures on which Britain's strength was principally built. Furthermore, few of these studies set out to illuminate the kind of problems we have been discussing—the nature of the environment which determined the entrepreneur's ambitions, his abilities, and the constraints within which he worked.

Comparisons of the kind made by Hoselitz and Landes are more instructive.[7] While they are not conclusive, they tend to confirm the view that social factors played an important part in determining the number of entrepreneurs and their characteristics. Thus Hoselitz finds that industrial entrepreneurship was more socially acceptable in Britain than in France in the eighteenth century. British entrepreneurs were drawn from a wider range of social backgrounds, which suggests perhaps a greater degree of social mobility and therefore a greater range of talent to draw upon. Also the political insecurity of the Huguenots in France restricted the kinds of investment they would undertake; and the long history of state initiative in France created a condition of 'industrial tutelage' in which the entrepreneur waited upon the initiative of the state rather than depending upon his own judgement.

Although these comparative studies are most useful they are essentially static. They are useful in suggesting what environmental influences are important. They may indicate the conditions in which entrepreneurship does or does not thrive. But they do not establish how a change from an unfavourable to a favourable environment occurs and how long such a change may take in different circumstances.

In addition to these specific studies of entrepreneurship there is also the longstanding debate about the effects of the Protestant ethic upon entrepreneurship—a debate we will return to in the next chapter. Apart from this there is at present little in historical study which tells us why entrepreneurial dynamism varied.

[7] See footnote 1 above.

THE NEED FOR STUDIES OF ENTREPRENEURIAL EMERGENCE

My proposal, which amounts to a plea for the study of the history of entrepreneurial emergence, has both difficulties and limitations. The first difficulty is to restrict the study to what is relevant, and in particular to trace and define limits. For instance, is the beginning of the emergence of British industrial entrepreneurship traceable to the commercial revolution of the seventeenth century, and if so what is the nature of the links with it? The problem is to distinguish between events which are contiguous with the development of industrial capitalism and events which are responsible for the conditions of the starting-point of the movement but which are not themselves directly connected.

The results of this study will not be directly applicable to today's problems because there are additional elements involved. Ideology can now play a much more decisive role in the process of entrepreneurial acceptance, and the skills of management so painfully built up by experience can now be acquired to some extent through business schools. Yet even here it may be highly dangerous to ignore environmental factors. We do not know how far the process of training is influenced by the kind of society in which the trainee has been raised. If, as seems likely, attitudes inculcated during childhood influence a person's mental processes, the training of business managers from underdeveloped communities may be a much more complex task than we imagine. And even when the training is completed, its full value will only be realized with experience. Clearly the very lack of development may limit opportunities for entrepreneurial experience in his own country, and experience in a developed economy is not necessarily relevant to the conditions under which he will work in his own country. It may well be that the production of an entrepreneurial class is in part a social process, and as such it may be evolutionary—geared to changes in society as a whole. The existence of an entrepreneurial or managerial group within an otherwise primitive economic community does not weigh against this point. The Quakers in seventeenth-century Britain or the Chinese in Malaya were in some measure divorced from the community at large. They were an enclave with a different tradition and ethos which was partly the cause of, and partly the result of, their social disenfranchisement. Thus the existence of this enclave does not necessarily disprove the contention that the emergence of managers and entrepreneurs is influenced by social environment. Nor does the existence of such a group remove the problem if it is necessary to produce entrepreneurs from a wide cross-section, though it may tend to minimize it.

SUBSTITUTES FOR ENTREPRENEURIAL INITIATIVE?

One interesting aspect of the entrepreneurial problem is the idea that it is possible to avoid the kind of motivational forces which drove Western entrepreneurs. Some argue that the Japanese avoided rapacious individualism by appealing to the national sentiments of possible entrepreneurs.[8] These scholars also seem to believe that the Japanese reduced the entrepreneurial problem by organizing on a large scale—in the Zaibatsu companies. It is outside our present scope to examine these propositions in the Japanese context, but it is true that many economists mirror these views, especially about the entrepreneurial-saving attributes of large-scale and government directed enterprise. I cannot pretend to make a comprehensive analysis of these propositions, but the British experience at least raises some thought-provoking issues.

There is considerable weight in the arguments of those favouring large-scale enterprises. These are preferred not simply because of supposed economies of scale but also because they will allow the most effective use of scarce resources: of management, entrepreneurship and finance. Moreover small-scale enterprises create special problems, such as the difficulty of organizing suitable financial institutions. There are complaints about the inadequacies of cheap finance for small businesses even in advanced and sophisticated economies. And how much more difficult is the organizational problem where the economy is under-developed; where the borrower may be inexperienced in organizing his affairs to keep his obligations under control; and where there are few experienced judges of leading risks? In short, the problems of financing small-scale business are multiplied where the community has little experience in handling commercially viable credit.

Nevertheless, we must seriously question the efficiency of large-scale enterprises in a community unaccustomed to big business. We must remember that many pre-industrial countries found large-scale enterprises inefficient and sluggish, often only maintained by an expensive system of government patronage (for mutual benefit, but not necessarily to the advantage of the economy at large) and liable to be associated with scandalous frauds and damaging manias.[9]

Now it is easy to assume that the faults of the early large enterprises were purely technical: that it was the deficiencies of the institutional framework or simply lack of expertise which throttled them. The immaturity of financial institutions in the eighteenth century encouraged the rash and speculative rather than the sound economic investment,

[8] G. Ranis, 1955; also B. Marshall, 1967 and J. Hirschmeier, 1964.
[9] S. Pollard, 1965, pp. 23 ff.

and this limited investors' sources of funds. As Professor Pollard demonstrates, the large-scale enterprise also requires special management skills of its own, and these early giants were not able to cope with such management problems.[10] It *may* be possible to solve problems of entrepreneurship by centralization; but this may create a shortage of lower-rank managers. It is by no means clear that it is easier to produce the right kind of manager than the right kind of entrepreneur. This is especially so when we realize that the theoretical distinction between a manager and an entrepreneur does not necessarily correspond with the names we commonly use. Managers of a large company or even a government enterprise must obviously perform entrepreneurial functions if the business is to succeed. Even the motivations of the 'manager' may be only superficially different from an independent entrepreneur. We must be careful not to define away a problem which will still be there in practice. Furthermore, it is by no means certain that governments and large institutions will provide the kind of dynamic leadership which an industrial transition requires.

It would be foolish to conclude that large-scale business should be excluded from development plans; indeed some activities require large businesses in the modern world. However, we should note that the large-scale businesses and the institutions surrounding them may not operate efficiently in a community with an unsuitable value system: where banks are not trusted, where workers are unaccustomed to the special disciplines of urban factory work, where the abstract incentives of a money economy are not appreciated, and so on. Moreover, it is unrealistic to expect large businesses to serve the whole economic structure. Some small and medium-scale enterprise is probably essential in a balanced economic framework. Concentrating exclusively on promoting large businesses may create a dual economy which does not produce the interplays which bring a regular progression towards industrialization. It seems almost certain that large businesses can only partly solve the scarcity problems of finance, entrepreneurship and management. A healthy long-run situation depends on producing a social climate which favours the *spontaneous* reaction by a dynamic entrepreneurial group to the needs and opportunities of economic growth.

INDUSTRIALIZATION AND THE WILLINGNESS TO INVEST

Let us now consider capital problems during industrialization. There are perhaps two key issues which interest British historians, first,

[10] *Ibid.*, pp. 15 ff. and 23 ff.

whether capital was a limiting factor in British economic growth and second, what influenced the supply of capital.

The first question has been the subject of occasional comment in broad treatments of the industrial revolution rather than of serious study. It seems a question of some importance, but it is perhaps as well that it has been neglected: it is surely impossible to answer. We would be safe in assuming that Britain's capacity to create capital would not have been sufficient to support industrialization in medieval times, and that this was no longer true by the end of the eighteenth century. Then when did the transition take place? The problem is not quite so simple as this formulation implies. For example, it would be surprising if capital shortage did not retard growth to some extent in the eighteenth century. If this is admitted, it becomes clear that the central issue is how *serious* capital shortage was at various stages, and whether it was ever sufficient to stifle growth potential. How do we begin to answer such a question? Perhaps we can rely upon the economists for guidance. Some economists tell us that investment must rise to ten or twelve per cent of national income.[11] However, these judgements are partly based on historical cases of growth so it would be tautological to rely upon them. Further, such judgements do not tell us whether the society was capable of raising its investments to that level some time earlier than it did. Moreover, there is the basic question of what a 'serious shortage of funds' means in this context. Does it mean perhaps that funds available are less than some optimum amount? But an optimum amount is only calculable on the basis of some predetermined or ideal economic structure. We are not likely to agree on what the economic structure could or should have been: we face the prospect of a 'counterfactual' bottomless pit.

Shortage can of course be determined from literary evidence, from the continual complaints of entrepreneurs; or perhaps can be inferred from the nature of financial institutions. But every economy will face shortages if these are the sole criteria. There are always entrepreneurs unsatisfied and institutional deficiences. Thus the problem is one of estimating the *extent* of the deficiency, if we are to pass judgement on whether it was or was not sufficient to stifle economic growth.

We must ask ourselves what we mean when we claim that there was no serious shortage of capital in eighteenth-century Britain. At best, the historian making such a claim is stating the obvious: that since Britain industrialized, she must have had the capital to do so. Historians who make comments on the adequacy of total capital supplies may well have been seduced by the emphasis of some economists on the 'vicious circle of poverty' in underdeveloped countries. This emphasizes the

[11] W. A. Lewis, 1955, p. 22–6; W. W. Rostow, 1960, p. 37.

simple fact that humans have a minimum consumption rate for survival and therefore that the technical ability to create capital depends upon the ability to produce above minimum survival levels. This is a truism, but it is not particularly helpful in analysing development problems because most people produce above the survival level. Indeed, economists in most cases are really talking, not about survival levels, but about a margin above subsistence levels. The difficulty is that subsistence does not mean the same thing to all peoples—what today's Australian would mean by a subsistence level is not what a Burmese would mean, nor even an Australian of twenty years ago.

The capacity to invest certainly depends upon the margin above survival levels, but it also depends upon what people choose to do with that margin—to raise consumption levels, to invest surplus cash, or to buy gold trinkets as a form of saving for adversity or old age. For development purposes it would be fruitful and interesting to explain the reasons why people vary in the uses to which they put their margin above survival level. To a large extent this is a product of attitudes.

What explains the variable willingness of people to invest? It varies between countries, as well as within a country over time; and it varies between one kind of investment and another. These variations occur because of differing opportunities, because of differing riskiness, and because of differing institutional efficiency in bringing opportunities before potential investors.

This is well enough understood. But current treatments tend to concentrate on the technical aspects of the relationships involved: opportunities vary because of the rate of growth of output; institutional efficiency is a technical or organizational efficiency. We tend to overlook the fact that opportunities, risk and institutional efficiency depend upon an attitudinal background. Attitudes can determine both the proportion of income devoted to investment and the uses to which investment capital is put. We must ask why men vary in their willingness to risk their capital, and why institutions differ in the confidence they command from people—because both are important determinants of investment levels, investment efficiency, and hence the growth of the economy. To some extent variable willingness to invest in risky enterprise is an indication and a consequence of variable entrepreneurial drive—it is the dynamic entrepreneur who is also the risk investor. But even in a relatively primitive economy such as in eighteenth-century Britain, it is not exactly the same thing. By no means all of the capital used by eighteenth-century British entrepreneurs was their own money. They could command outside funds and this was probably an important element in British growth—an element which should be explained.

CAPITAL AND CAPITAL SOURCES IN BRITAIN

Present studies of financial institutions during the industrial revolution are often disappointing because their emphasis is upon the history of modern institutions. Thus many current studies investigate the history of banking. Banking in the eighteenth century was obviously import-ant in money exchange—which was essential to the growth of the economy—and this is not to be forgotten. On the other hand, it appears that banks played an insignificant part in mobilizing funds for invest-ment. This is not a novel judgement, though it is not based on the traditional view of the role of banks. It has long been argued that the banks did not play a significant part in the industrial revolution because they did not lend to industrialists on a long-term basis, and therefore they were not important in providing funds for new kinds of invest-ment.[12] This is probably true but in a sense only a technical quibble, because they did provide working capital to industrialists and this may have allowed the industrialists to concentrate their own funds upon providing the new fixed equipment. Indeed, the argument can be pushed further because it is obvious that investment in fixed industrial equipment was only one aspect of the essential capital requirements of growth—it was just as essential that capital should be mobilized for improving agriculture, transport and mines, and even the construction of cities. Thus one may believe that the literature concentrates excess-ively upon one aspect of capital requirements for growth. Moreover, Pollard[13] warns us that we may have to look beyond current accounting concepts when assessing the industrialist's capital arrangements. He explains how industrialists often used short-term borrowing for fixed capital construction, using their own employees—whose pay they delayed—to build equipment from materials they obtained on normal mercantile credit. It is true that Pollard has not demonstrated how extensive this conversion of circulating capital into fixed assets may have been in the eighteenth century, but he has certainly opened an interesting line of thought which adds weight to the idea that the tradi-tional approach concentrates too much on one particular type of invest-ment.

However, my judgement of the significance of banks in providing capital is on quite different lines, based on a simple estimate of the proportion of new savings which the banks may have mobilized. The level of credit creation by the banks is estimated for the nineteenth century by adding deposits in trading and savings banks to note circula-

[12] M. M. Postan, 1935–6.
[13] S. Pollard, 1964b.

tion as a rough indication of total funds available for investment, deducting twenty per cent from this for cash reserves.[14] We have no similar figures for the early eighteenth century, so we must use the early nineteenth-century figures as an upper limit for the increase in bank credit creation over the century. These results are compared with changes in capital stock, using estimates from various sources.[15] The results are extremely rough, but they suggest that banks played a very minor role indeed in supplying funds for net additions to capital. Between 1688 and the early nineteenth century, bank lending ran at only three to five per cent of the increase in national capital. Even in the nineteenth century the contribution of banks rose very slowly. Except for the short period 1800–12, the proportion of capital funds supplied by bank credit creation did not rise above ten per cent until after 1885. The result for 1800–12 is largely because bank deposits were unusually high in 1812: they fell subsequently and did not rise to the 1812 level again until more than twenty years later.

In the U.S.A., in contrast to Britain, banks played a much larger part in the transition phase. There, banks may have contributed nearly eleven per cent to the increased funds devoted to capital formation between 1869 and 1909.[16]

The stock and share market is an even more important institutional source of funds in the modern world but, as is well known, public flotations played very little part in the early phases of the industrial revolution—except perhaps for canal and turnpike construction. Incorporation was made expensive and difficult after the frauds and speculative bubbles of the early eighteenth century. This position was only gradually whittled away by the Acts of 1826, 1833, 1855 and 1862. Pressnell observes that the 1708 Act prohibiting joint stock banking, except for the Bank of England, was probably justified in the circumstances, though its effects were felt well after the need for restriction had passed.[17] This judgement raises the question of how to assess the effects of the restriction and just when the need for restriction had passed.

Another thread of modern studies is the improvement in government finance. A. H. John argues that this was not only important in itself: it was also the basis of an expanding money market.[18] Government borrowing may have been an element in an improved money market, but in the context of the eighteenth century it may not have had a significant effect on capital formation. Unlike modern govern-

---

[14] J. K. Horsefield, 1960, pp. 261, 263 f.
[15] See Appendix, p. 146.
[16] U.S. Department of Commerce, 1949, sections A, N; and S. Kuznets, 1961, Table 3.
[17] L. S. Pressnell, 1956, pp. 5–6.
[18] A. H. John, 1953; see also P. G. M. Dickson, 1967, pp. 11–12.

ments, those of the eighteenth century played a minimal part in the economy. Their borrowings were chiefly used to finance wars which had little direct significance for capital formation—though the expenditure on wars may have had indirect effects by raising the level of demand and by strengthening Britain's position in important markets.

Nor is the general money market likely to have been greatly swollen by the improved standing of government bonds as John suggests. He does not explain the mechanics of the relationship between expanding credit and more secure government bonds. It would hardly have any appreciable effect upon commercial credit, as this was organizationally well advanced. Possibly government borrowing now drew upon savings which were previously hoarded. This may have had little direct effect upon the general capital market because the new, careful investor would not be likely to use his bonds as backing for other ventures. However, the effect may have been indirect—the new sources of funds pushed down government bond interest rates, which perhaps persuaded the adventurous to turn from government bonds to other investments. Those who previously sought high returns by lending to government, accepting the high risks, may now have been forced into the commercial market to find that kind of investment.[19] Hence stability in government finances may have increased capital entering the general market. From what we know of the ways in which capital was raised in the eighteenth century it is unlikely that this was a major source of funds, because of the weakness of financial institutions which could organize semi-speculative investments.

It seems that much of the literature on financial matters is too concerned with the evolution of modern institutions in the British economy. This is not to argue against the importance of these studies for other purposes—since Britain was the cradle from which a healthy child sprang to influence much of the world. However, for our present purpose it is necessary to study the growth of self-finance, loans on a personal basis and merchant financing, in addition to studies of banks, joint stock companies and government finance. These studies will also have to be cross-classified according to various types of enterprise: it is not necessarily relevant to industrialists and merchants that funds for canal building can be raised by public subscription in the eighteenth century.

Nor should we draw too much from short-run cases. The speculations of the early eighteenth century possibly indicate only that people are prepared to invest temporarily in non-personal loans for immediate speculative gain. Such an attitude is not necessarily the basis of an

---

[19] See P. G. M. Dickson, 1967, Ch. 19, which contains evidence both for and against this proposition.

economy in which non-personal loans can supply a large bulk of funds for permanent investment in economic enterprises.

Thinking in terms of aggregates is one of the deficiencies of present historical judgements about British capital sources. For instance, some see the rapidity of the rebuilding of London after the Great Fire or the fall in interest rates in the eighteenth century as an indication that there was no shortage of capital. However, the fall in interest rates was on government loans; they must have been especially influenced by the financial reforms of the 1720s which reduced the risks of lending to government. This is hardly relevant to the market's judgement of risk in novel enterprises associated with the industrial revolution. Nor is a once-and-for-all mustering of capital, such as was involved in rebuilding London, necessarily an indication that the economy is capable of a sustained high rate of investment. It may be that the funds for the rebuilding were drawn from hoarded wealth, and that annual increments to the wealth *may* have been relatively small. Isolated evidence such as this does not show that capital would have been available for new kinds of economic venture. Nor does the money available for the South Sea Bubble indicate that a stock market could have been established in the eighteenth century with better under-standing of stock exchange organization. Money for speculation is not necessarily money which can be mobilized for industry—or a. r other long-term investment venture. Certainly, if we examine rather primitive expedients used by many industrialists in the eighteenth century, it is difficult to believe that there were no capital problems.

Thus studies of eighteenth-century British capital sources are in an unsatisfactory state partly because they are conducted in terms of modern financial institutions, rather than in terms of the financial system as it existed in the eighteenth century. But they are also unsatisfactory because they fail to consider the attitudinal background to changing financial arrangements. How and when did various sections of the com-munity come to accept the risks and recognize the benefits of personal and non-personal lending for building factories and machines, roads and canals, houses and shops? How long did it take the people to under-stand and accept institutional methods of drawing funds from those who had them, to be used productively by those who had the will and ability to use them? We must try to build up a picture of the attitudes which underlay investment, and the *changing* attitudes which underlay expanding investment and new forms of investment. It is a mistake to assume that attitudes towards investment and financial institutions can be transformed overnight. Historians' studies of these underlying attitudes may give some clues about how protracted and difficult such transformation is likely to be.

I would emphasize, too, that for our purposes this is not just a problem of totals of consumption and saving. Sufficient funds for one sector, and willingness to invest funds in that sector, do not indicate willingness to invest in others. The problem of discovering whether attitudes restricted the quantity of investment funds is not an aggregate problem. Who can suppose that capital markets for commerce, agriculture, industry, housing, banking and transport are one and the same? Minority groups have often been willing to invest substantial sums in commerce, but not in illiquid industrial plant.[20]

FURTHER READING

On finance and capital:

ASHTON, T. S.: *The Industrial Revolution 1760–1830.* (Chs. 1 and 4)

ASHTON, T. S. and SAYERS, R. S.: *Papers in English Monetary History.*

CAMERON, RONDO *et al*: *Banking in the Early Stages of Industrialization: A Study in Comparative Economic History.*

DEANE, PHYLLIS: 'The Implications of Early National Income Estimates for the Measurement of Long-term Economic Growth in the United Kingdom'.

'The Industrial Revolution and Economic Growth: The Evidence of Early British National Income Estimates'.

'Capital Formation in Britain before the Railway Age'.

DICKSON, P. G. N.: *The Financial Revolution in England.*

FLINN, M. W.: *The Origins of the Industrial Revolution.* (Ch. 3)

HIGGINS, J. P. P. and POLLARD, S.: *Aspects of Capital Investment in Great Britain 1750–1850.*

JOHN, A. H.: 'Insurance Investment and the London Money Market of the Eighteenth Century'.

JOSLIN, D. M.: 'London Private Bankers 1720–85'.

MATHIAS, PETER: *The First Industrial Nation.* (Ch. 4)

POSTAN, M. M.: 'Recent Trends in the Accumulation of Capital'.

POLLARD, S.: 'Capital Accounting in the Industrial Revolution'.

'Fixed Capital in the Industrial Revolution in Britain'.

PRESSNELL, L. S.: 'Public Monies and the Development of English Banking'.

Country Banking in the Industrial Revolution.

'The Rate of Interest in the Eighteenth Century'.

SHANNON, H. A.: 'The Coming of General Limited Liability'.

SHAPIRO, SEYMOUR: *Capital and the Cotton Industry in the Industrial Revolution.*

[20] E. Hagen, 1962a, pp. 18 ff.; B. E. Supple, 1961, p. 474.

On entrepreneurship:

AITKEN, HUGH (ed.): *Explorations in Enterprise.*

GERSCHENKRON, A.: 'Social Attitudes, Entrepreneurship, and Economic Development'.

'Some Further Notes on Social Attitudes, Entrepreneurship, and Economic Development'.

'The Modernization of Entrepreneurship'.

HABAKKUK, H. J.: 'Economic Functions of English Landowners in the Seventeenth and Eighteenth Centuries'.

HARBISON, F. H. and MYERS, C. A.: *Management in the Industrial World.*

HOSELITZ, B. F.: 'Entrepreneurship and Capital Formation in France and Britain since 1700'.

'Entrepreneurship and Economic Growth'; 'Social Structure and Economic Growth'; and 'A Sociological Approach to Economic Development'.

HAGEN, E.: 'A Framework for Analysing Economic and Political Change'.

LANDES, D.: 'French Entrepreneurship and Industrial Growth in the Nineteenth Century'.

'French Business and Businessmen: A Social and Cultural Analysis'.

'Social Attitudes, Entrepreneurship, and Economic Development'.

MCKENDRICK, N.: 'Josiah Wedgwood: An Eighteenth-century Entrepreneur in Salesmanship and Marketing Techniques'.

POLLARD, S.: 'Factory Discipline in the Industrial Revolution'.

The Genesis of Modern Management.

RANIS, G.: 'The Community-centred Entrepreneur in Japanese Development'.

REDLICH, F.: 'Business Leadership: Diverse Origins and Variant Forms'.

ROBINSON, E.: 'Eighteenth-century Commerce and Fashion: Matthew Boulton's Marketing Techniques'.

SAWYER, J. E.: 'The Entrepreneur and the Social Order: France and the United States'.

'Strains in the Social Structure of Modern France'.

SOLTOW, J.: 'The Entrepreneur in Economic History'.

SUPPLE, B. A.: 'Economic History and Economic Underdevelopment'.

WILSON, C.: 'The Entrepreneur in the Industrial Revolution in Britain'.

8 Religion and the Social Environment

There is a growing literature on how differences in social systems influence economic performance. Such differences have been used, for instance, to explain why Japan has become a highly industrialized country while Thailand has remained comparatively underdeveloped.[1] Yet if much is being made of these differences, very little is done to explain how the differences came about—how and why attitudes conducive to industrialization came to be established in some societies and not others. The growing emphasis by economists upon attitudes is now a further spur to overcome the historians' neglect.

One historically relevant issue is the Weber thesis,[2] which postulates a positive relationship between the Protestant ethic emerging from the Reformation and the rise of the spirit of capitalism. However it is not an easy thesis to follow, as the voluminous literature testifies. Further, Weber's approach revolves around only one aspect of entrepreneurship, and there are clearly many other social and intellectual influences upon industrialization. Perhaps Weber's thesis could be made to explain some others, such as why workman accepted factory discipline and a new regularity of work. But there are other social influences on the economy. Social factors may determine whether men accept money as a measure and store of value, and whether they are prepared to invest in a public company with its abstraction from personalities. Social factors also influence men's occupational mobility; their attitudes to authority and individual initiative; whether they believed they control their economic lives—as opposed to the fatalistic attitude of men who see the weather as the over-riding controller of their lives—etc. Just what is involved in the individualism and materialism of Western culture is of course not entirely clear, but what is clear is that Weber's work is circumscribed. And yet there is little doubt that the thesis is relevant to part of the field—a field which is otherwise neglected.

The issue central to the Weber approach is accumulation of capital: the emphasis upon new attitudes to work (calling) and savings (thrifti-

[1] E. B. Ayal, 1963.
[2] Max Weber, 1930.

ness) is economically relevant to the creation of a surplus above current consumption, which is then presumably available for investment. There is, of course, no reason to suppose that to work harder and save more will necessarily affect investment unless we are talking in Keynesian *ex post* terms. The incentive to invest does not depend simply on whether money is available. Nevertheless, any influences upon entrepreneurs should be carefully examined, especially in an age when most promoters and managers are also investors. Institutions did not play a major role in providing new capital in Britain, and thus the role of the entrepreneur was critical. There are other reasons for studying religion, particularly because of its influence on social aspirations generally. It is probably true that all peoples dream of being richer, but actively pursuing wealth often conflicts with other social and cultural aspirations. The problem for the economist is not to create the desire for more wealth but to tip the scale of social values more in its favour. Since the level of economic effort is clearly influenced by the balance of social values, and since religion is part of the value system, there is a strong case for studying religious change.

Scholars involved in the Protestant ethic debate commonly try to establish a linear causal relationship. They seek either to establish that changing religion influenced economic life, or the opposite relationship—that the growth of the economy changed religious attitudes in economic matters. One notable exception is R. H. Tawney[3] who argues, correctly, for a mutual interaction. Broadly it seems clear that the great change in the power and the teachings of religion between the beginning of the Reformation and the eighteenth century must have profoundly influenced the value system of the community. At the same time there is strong evidence of a reverse influence, i.e. that economic change brought a slow but fundamental response from the religious community.

While Tawney seems to stand above others in this aspect of his interpretation, his analysis of the influence of religion upon economic life follows the conventional pattern. He follows Weber in emphasizing the positive influence of the Protestant ethic upon work, and his evidence and methods are in the Weberian mould.

The literature upon the Weber thesis is now voluminous and indeterminate. No doubt this is partly because of the nature of the problem, in that we are dealing with 'intangibles', but it is also largely the outcome of the methodology used. This methodology is the descendant of the approach which Weber used over half a century ago. Its outstanding feature is that it is indirect—in the sense that it is two stages removed from the starting point of the problem. We are primarily

[3] R. H. Tawney, 2nd edn., 1937.

concerned to examine the way in which community attitudes towards economic matters altered, and to judge the influence of these attitudes upon the working of the economic system. This includes not only the economic attitudes of community leaders—which may for example influence government policy—but also, and perhaps most importantly, the economic attitudes of the middle and lower classes.

Weber and his followers find most of their inspiration and evidence in the pronouncements of the great religious leaders like Calvin, Luther, Baxter and Wesley. However, there are two stages of interpretation between the beliefs of the ordinary people and the pronouncements of the great leaders: the ordinary pastor's interpretation of what his leader has said, and the layman's interpretation of what the pastor has said. This may not seem of great importance—indeed, the assumption that we can discern the attitudes of the layman by examining the leader's pronouncement is plausible enough on the surface—but in fact this methodology may seriously distort the true picture.

First, the pastor may have interpreted the leader's pronouncements according to the circumstances which he faced at parish level. In the U.S.A. during the nineteenth century, I. G. Wyllie found that clergy were tolerant of riches and rich men in the wealthy city communities, but not in rural districts.[4] I would argue that the great leaders were well aware that circumstances must shape specific judgements, and as a consequence their pronouncements were usually highly generalized. John Wesley, for example, often referred to economic matters in his sermons, but as a rule his pronouncements were very general. His favourite phrases were 'gain all you can' and 'save all you can' but 'give all you can'.[5] On the few occasions when he felt constrained to explain these phrases, he was inclined to rhetorical answers that were surely not intended to be taken literally; if they were, they were certainly not capitalistic in spirit. Thus he said, the sin of avarice applies to 'all those that calmly, deliberately, and of set purpose, *endeavour* after more than food and coverings'.[6] On giving, he said: 'I do not say "Be a good Jew; giving a tenth of all you possess." I do not say, "Be a good Pharisee; giving a fifth of all your substance." I dare not advise you to give half of what you have; no, nor three quarters; but all!'[7] In a calmer mood he replied to a layman who asked for guidance: 'It is impossible to lay down any general rules, as to "saving all we can" and "giving all we can". In this, it seems, we must needs be directed, from time to time, by the

[4] I. G. Wyllie, *The Self-Made Man in America: the Myth of Rags to Riches*, Rutgers University Press, New Brunswick, N. J. (1954), quoted in Kurt Samuelsson, 1961, pp. 68–9.
[5] John Wesley, 1872, Vol. VII, pp. 8, 361; see also *Arminian Magazine*, Vol. X, 1787, pp. 155–6.
[6] John Wesley, 1872, Vol. VII, p. 3.   [7] *Ibid.*, Vol. VII, pp. 9–10.

unction of the Holy One.'[8] This illustrates Wesley's realization that all surrounding circumstances must be considered before general principles could be translated into specific rules; but it also shows that there must have been a large gap between parishoner and great leader—which was usually filled by the local pastor.

Current method interposes the modern historian into the interpretative gaps. This assumes firstly that the modern mind will interpret what is said in the same way as the man of that day would interpret it. This is a highly dangerous assumption in itself, since on this issue an interpretation often depends upon a delicate balance of counterpoised positions. For instance, leaders often lauded thrift and hard work but condemned deliberate seeking of wealth. How the individual reconciles these into an intelligible ethos clearly depends upon his interpretation of the meaning of words and on the balance between partly conflicting ideas. For the modern historian to place himself in the position of interpreter is to imply similar thought patterns to the contemporary, as well as similar background knowledge influencing his interpretation of a particular piece of information. Clearly these are dangerous assumptions at such a distance in time. Even modern scholars, without a gulf of time and environment dividing them, differ markedly over interpretation. Some see the essence of Wesley's teaching in one passage, while others quote to an exactly opposite effect. For instance, when Wesley said that a man should gain all he can and save all he can, he invariably linked those with giving all he can. Where did his emphasis lie? What did he have in mind in making these points? It is certainly possible to quote in apparent support of the concept of calling. A Christian must work to please God: 'He works for eternity.'[9] But perhaps his emphasis was upon effort rather than achievement, '. . . sloth being inconsistent with religion'.[10] Or the balance of meaning and emphasis may be changed by other quotes: 'But as zealous as we are for all good works, we should still be more zealous for holy tempers— lowliness of mind, meekness, gentleness, longsuffering, contentedness, resignation unto the will of God, deadness to the world and the things of the world, as the only means of being truly alive to God[11] [and] . . . most zealous of all, for that which is the sum and perfection of religion, the *love* of God and man.'[12] It is difficult to argue from this pronouncement that the concept of calling was central to Methodist ideals—as it is difficult to see it in statements such as 'faith is the only *condition* of justification'.[13]

Now problems of semantics and balance of meaning may be un-

[8] *Ibid.*, Vol. XII, p. 301.
[9] *Ibid.*, Vol. VII, p. 31.
[10] *Ibid.*, Vol. VII, p. 31.

[11] *Ibid.*, Vol. VII, pp. 61–2.
[12] *Ibid.*, Vol. VII, p. 65.
[13] *Ibid.*, Vol. V, p. 62.

avoidable in a topic such as this. Here the problems are compounded, because the dispute amongst modern scholars is more than a dispute amongst contemporaries about the meaning of words; it is a dispute about interpreting words as eighteenth-century men would interpret them in an environment, of course, profoundly different from our own. We are not only disagreeing about the meaning of words; we are also disagreeing about what they mean to other men. It might be said quite seriously that each of us is arguing: 'Most men in the eighteenth century would have thought like me when they read these words, not like you.'

Apart from the problem of interpretation and practical meaning, this methodology also implies that the pronouncements of key religious leaders had universal influence at the time. The most important issue may not be whether particular attitudes were present or absent in a community, but who held these attitudes. What classes of the community held 'commercial' attitudes at any time, and how did the rest of the community view these attitudes? There was probably little difference in the commercial attitudes of a Medici or a Rockefeller, but the community which surrounded them was probably markedly different (if the agrarian sectors are included in that community). Further we must note the simple point that many religious leaders, such as Wesley, were not addressing the whole community, and would not be heeded by the whole community. Often they were addressing minority groups.

Moreover there is the simple question of the importance of economic matters: were they central or peripheral to the interests of the leader and to the people who listened? The importance of a particular statement therefore depends upon whom the religious leader was addressing, who was prepared to listen, how much notice they took, and so on. Since the analysis extends over at least three centuries, it is obviously implausible to assume that religious leaders will reflect or shape attitudes of the whole community, or even of any one class in that community, for the whole time. This would imply that the pronouncements of the great religious leaders were the only significant influence upon men's economic attitudes. This is particularly unlikely in an age of growing secularization, which certainly describes the period between the Reformation and the eighteenth century. The implicit assumption that the pronouncements of religious leaders will reflect community attitudes —or will exactly *shape* community thinking—is plainly much too sweeping.

Thus for various reasons the ideas of the great religious leaders may have been distorted or variously interpreted by ordinary men according to their preconceptions and the kind of community in which they lived. We have noted how general the great leaders' pronouncements tended to be; the Weberian interpretation assumes uniformity in converting these general statements into practical rules and standards of daily conduct. This is poor methodology and especially inexplicable in the light of Weber's treatment of Calvinism. He argues that the Protestant ethic developed despite Calvin's specific injunctions against seeking wealth; and he further argues that the Calvinists distorted Calvin's doctrine of predestination.[14] Somewhere between Calvin himself and grass-roots Calvinism, as it developed, the essence of Calvin's message was completely transformed. This implies that it would be a mistake to examine Calvin's attitudes as a test of community attitudes. Why then should we accept Weber's implicit assumption that the ideas of Baxter, Spencer, Barclay, Wesley, etc., were not similarly transformed? Why should we assume that their ideas are mirrored in the ideas of all their followers?

If it is true that the problem is to define precisely not only what views were held but also who held them, it seems clear that only a direct approach will be satisfactory. Although it is more convenient to study the writings of a few influential leaders, many things stood between these writings and the actual attitudes of ordinary men. This does not mean that studies are irrelevant, since we also want to know what factors may have been responsible for changing attitudes, and religious leaders certainly may have been influential. However, it is putting the cart before the horse to examine their writings as an index of changing economic attitudes in the community. Even careful re-phrasing does not alter this judgement. If the main question is whether religious change altered economic attitudes, correct methodology requires us to discover first whether economic attitudes did alter and exactly how they altered. The present approach compounds the problems of interpretation—on a question which is inherently complex—as well as opening the door to circular reasoning.

RELIGIOUS CHANGE AND THE RISE OF EUROPEAN CAPITALISM

All this is, however, an objection not so much to the Weber thesis as such as to the method of examining it—to the kind of evidence brought to bear upon it. It goes no way towards disproving the thesis, though it discounts the proof that has been offered. There are other problems with Weber's work. There is the problem of appreciation—the exact nature of the thesis—as well as the problem of seeing precisely how the Protestant ethic affected the working of the economy.

What were the essential attributes of the Protestant ethic as Weber

14 Max Weber, 1930, pp. 110–12.

saw it? To begin with we must notice that it is not a thesis of social approval.[15] It is not simply that the environment became more conducive to economic freedom and liberalism: 'it was not just the ability of people to free oneself from a common tradition.' Peacock[16] says that Weber emphasized that the Calvinists condemned wealth even more strongly than the Catholics. The consequence of Calvinist teachings arose from a subtle psychological effect of the concept of calling allied with the concept of thrift. The effect of this alliance was so subtle that the result was exactly the opposite of what the Calvinists sought in economic matters—the avoidance of great wealth.

In essence the Weber thesis seems simple enough: that the concept of calling persuaded men to apply themselves with great energy to their jobs, thereby increasing their incomes. At the same time the Puritans emphasized living thriftly and avoiding luxury which caused them to save rather than spend their additional incomes; hence funds were accumulated for investment. Delving deeper, however, we discover that Weber's concept of calling is more complex than this simple formulation suggests.

It seems obvious, for instance, that the Puritan groups were not the only ones to emphasize work in the service of God. Samuelsson shows that the Catholics had a similar concept.[17] Christopher Hill argues that the central target of the reformers' attack was justification by works.[18] Samuelsson has pointed out that the idea of good works is not necessarily the same as hard work in one's daily job as part of the service to God; but it is clear enough that the Puritans had no monopoly even in the latter idea. Thus in Weber we find that the concept of calling is said to have originated with Luther,[19] and yet Lutheranism is excluded from Weber's Protestant ethic. Weber argued that Luther had other ideas which were anti-capitalistic, and that consequently the practical effects of his ideas on 'calling' were neutralized.[20] It is therefore clear that the concept of calling involves more than just acceptance of the idea of daily hard work in the service of God. Was it simply that the Puritans gave more emphasis to this idea, or that other elements were combined with the idea? One can get evidence for both points of view from Weber. First, Weber might say that the idea of daily effort in the service of God was central to the Puritan doctrine, but was only part of Catholic doctrine. It became central to the salvation of the Puritan because he saw nothing standing between him and God. There was a direct rela-

[15] Max Weber, 1930, pp. 70–78.
[16] J. L. Peacock, 1969, p. 36.
[17] K. Samuelsson, 1961, pp. 17 ff.
[18] Christopher Hill, 1961, p. 16.
[19] Max Weber, 1930, p. 80.
[20] *Ibid.*, pp. 82–6.

tionship with God and *only* a direct relationship, which was also a constant or daily relationship. Hence the ordinary life of the Puritan became central to his communication with God and thus central to his salvation. On the other hand the Church was interposed between the Catholic and God, and God's judgement of a man could be ameliorated or dampened by the Church. Hence for the Catholic, daily effort in the service of God was less important because his main relationship with God was through the Church, in contrast to the direct relationship of the Puritans.[21] This argument perhaps establishes a difference in the importance of the concept to the Catholic as compared with the Puritan, but it does not explain the difference between Lutheran and Puritan.

This can only be explained by some other elements combined with the idea of calling. Thus Weber emphasizes the importance of profits to Puritans—'if . . . God, whose hand the Puritan sees in all the occurrences of life, shows one of His elect a chance of profit, he [God] must do it with a purpose . . . if you refuse this, and choose the less gainful way, you cross one of the ends of your calling, and you refuse to be God's steward.'[22] This is in startling contrast to Weber's emphasis on the strength of Calvin's condemnation of wealth. Just how and when was 'daily effort for salvation' translated into pursuit of profit? The Calvinists' pursuit of profit and the most profitable occupation appear to be crucial aspects of Weber's concept of calling, but they are not clearly explained and analysed. His emphasis on the pursuit of profit also rests somewhat uneasily beside his interpretation of the effect of the Protestant ethic upon the working classes[23]—they were led to work harder but to seek little return and to be satisfied with their position in life. Hence Weber argues that the ethic increased the employer's avidity for profit, but caused his workers to increase their productive efforts selflessly—with obvious consequences for rates of profit. The contrast between the effect of the ethic on the quiescent worker as opposed to the driving entrepreneur is remarkable, but Weber makes no effort to reconcile them, nor does he offer much evidence of substance to establish and explain this remarkable dichotomy.

A further puzzling aspect of Weber is his idea that religious zeal impelled the Puritan to action, but that once the action was under way religious principle was laid aside and the Puritan businessman became ruthless and without conscience.[24] The Puritan was apparently afflicted by a bad conscience if he slacked, but not if he avidly applied unfair business methods. And yet one of the most striking aspects of post-

[21] *Ibid.*, pp. 115–20.
[22] *Ibid.*, p. 162.
[23] *Ibid.*, pp. 177–9.
[24] *Ibid.*, p. 151.

Reformation economic attitudes was the increasing emphasis upon the rule of conscience—a point we will return to later.

In summary, then, it seems that Weber has not drawn a clear distinction between the Protestant ethic and the ethics of other religious groups. All had an element of working in the service of God, of condemnation of wealth. No doubt there were differences of emphasis upon these things in the ethics of different groups—as well as in the same group at different times—but these are differences of degree, not of kind. It is Weber's effort to show that there was a positive element in the Protestant ethic, an element either new or unique—and thus a difference in kind—that is suspect. Perhaps Weber's conclusion that the Protestant ethic was conducive to capitalism is acceptable if based on an argument that the balance of this ethic was somewhat more tolerant of economic efforts than others; but this is a social acceptance thesis which apparently Weber rejects.

Moreover, even if one can dispel all doubts about the schizophrenic and selective psychological effects of the Protestant ethic, there remains the question of how it came to produce a pervasive 'national character'. What were the mechanisms of transfer, from the minority Puritan groups to the remainder of the population, from Protestant to Catholic countries, and to an era when the capitalistic spirit was no longer backed by religious zeal?

In many communities the Protestant sects, as Weber defines them, were minority groups and often disestablished groups: for example the Quakers were precluded from holding public office in England. One of the most puzzling aspects of the Weber thesis is how the views of the Puritans came to predominate in the community: how their views came to form the basis of 'the *ethos* of an economic system'.[25] Weber, of course, does not deny other influences upon the spirit of capitalism, but if the Protestant ethic was a predominant influence it must have been transmitted to the majority in some way, directly or indirectly. Peacock's exposition of Weber's doctrine argues that the ethic drove men to both entrepreneurial action and the creation of a capitalistic social order, and that 'modern life is built around institutions which sustain capitalism'.[26] It is clear that if the Protestant ethic was as important to the rise of the spirit of capitalism as Weber suggests, the quintessence of the ethic must have been transmitted to other sections of the community. If the Protestants supplied a disproportionate number of entrepreneurs[27] they did not supply all, and it is unquestionably true that the spirit of capitalism deeply penetrated

[25] Max Weber, 1930, p. 27.
[26] J. L. Peacock, 1969, p. 37.
[27] Even this has been questioned—see C. M. Elliott, 1967.

non-Puritan sections of society. How then was the spirit transmitted? If the achievements of the Puritans persuaded others to follow them, we might expect a radical improvement in the Puritans' social position as they became admired paragons of social virtue rather than outcasts. At the very least we might expect their numbers to be greatly swelled at the expense of other groups as the virtues of their outlook were realized. But there is little evidence of this in eighteenth-century England. Indeed, the large number of new religious groups indicates dissatisfaction with existing sects rather than attraction towards them. Together Weber's Puritan sects probably increased their influence, but the 'Puritans' of the seventeenth century did not, and all Puritan sects combined would still be very much in the minority. Further, how was the ethic transmitted to Catholic Belgium—believed by some to be the second country to pass through an industrial revolution?

A rather more subtle problem, but no less important, is how the spirit transmitted itself once the religious basis died away. Weber admits that the religious backing to these materialistic ideas had disappeared by the time of Benjamin Franklin. Indeed, he argues that '. . . the full economic effect of those great religious movements . . . generally came only after the peak of purely religious enthusiasm was past'.[28] This is a curious characteristic of a major influence upon the economic ethos, which in itself raises some doubts about the whole thesis, but leaving that aside, exactly how was the impulse transmitted to the later age? Weber's explanation is that the spirit of capitalism came to feed upon its own success. A parallel on an individual level is perhaps found in Weber's idea that the rising middle class tended to repudiate the old ideas as its wealth accumulated.[29]

In view of this explanation it is somewhat surprising that Weber uses Franklin as the epitome of the capitalistic spirit in the eighteenth century. Franklin lived in the U.S.A., which Weber describes as a primitive economy at this time—a point which he uses to demonstrate his argument that the capitalistic spirit cannot be regarded as a reflection of material conditions.[30] We are left wondering, then, why the spirit of capitalism survived in the eighteenth-century U.S.A. If the religious backing had died away and it was still a primitive economy' it would seem that there was no success for the ethic to feed upon, so why did it survive? In Holland, Weber says, Calvinism held full sway for only seven years, and then its purity was perverted by sensualism and idolatry of the flesh.[31] Are we to believe that the impulse of these seven years

[28] Max Weber, 1930, p. 176.
[29] *Ibid.*, pp. 176–80.
[30] *Ibid.*, pp. 74–5.
[31] *Ibid.*, pp. 172–3.

imbued the Dutch with a capitalistic spirit which carried them to the height of economic power in the seventeenth century? Surely other influences must have been at work; and if so, it becomes a question of the relative significance of the Puritan influence during those seven years compared with other influences.

We have tried to clarify Weber's concept of calling, and we have puzzled over how this concept was transmitted to non-Puritan peoples and to non-Puritan times. Perhaps a more fundamental question is what part Weber's concept has in the acquisitive spirit as a whole: what perspective does it have in the community's total attitude towards business and work? There are at least four different aspects of social influences upon economic activities of the individual. First, the social standing of the businessman may affect the number of businessmen available, and the range of social classes from which business talent is likely to come. Second, there may be social constraints upon business methods. Usury laws, guild regulations, trade union activities, community attitudes towards automation, all put limits upon the business practices of businessmen. Third, the motives of the businessmen may be shaped by community attitudes. Although economists normally assume that businessmen attempt to maximize profits, we know that other motives often modify this aim. Nepotism would be one such modifying influence. Some businessmen have a pride in the quality of the product, which modifies profit-seeking practice. Apart from these extraneous factors that tend to erode a pure profit motive, we know that the intensity of the drive to make money varies among businessmen. Fourth, the *worker's* attitude to work may also vary.

We should note that Weber's concern is mainly with the third of these four factors—social influence on the motives of entrepreneurs—and even there with only one aspect of social influence: that is the drive to make profits. Even if Weber is right in arguing that the Protestant ethic caused businessmen to strive harder to make profits, the economic consequences surely depended upon other aspects of the social environment mentioned. The overall economic effect of a more intense drive for profits would depend on whether some occupations remained beyond the pale, whether there were any serious social or legal restrictions on business methods, and so on. Although Weber is most concerned with the drive to make profits, he appears to be aware that these other social factors were involved in the historical process he analyses. They are woven into his analysis, though they are not clearly distinguished from the concept of calling and the interrelationships between the various factors are not analysed. Thus Weber admits that the Church had been moving towards 'acceptance of capitalistic business forms', but adds that one of the reasons why it had been equivocal was its fear of collision with the usury laws.[32] Here is a hint that there was growing toleration of businessmen and relaxation of attitudes towards business methods. One may argue that both were essential to the worldly success of the idea of calling. What effect would the idea of calling have had if it had not been for the growing importance of non-agrarian occupations? The rise of these occupations was, of course, dependent upon attitudes towards them: upon the rising status of the merchant class, for instance. Further, the effect of the new work ethic would have been immeasurably reduced if it had been applied in a medieval atmosphere. If the usury laws had been applied with full force, and guild regulations strictly enforced, the new ethic would have had limited consequences. Weber, of course, argues that the Protestant churches were advanced in both these respects, but he does not explain why this was so. The changing attitudes towards business and businessmen do not seem a necessary consequence of the idea of a calling. Did the Protestant ethic urge men to change their minds about the kinds of legitimate business practices and the kinds of socially acceptable occupations? Weber does not come to grips with these questions. He offers little evidence that the attitudes of the Protestants towards these things differed markedly from those of other groups, and even less to show that any changes were a positive result of changing theology. Weber's idea that society was transformed by the concept of calling therefore rests upon some important social changes which claim little of his attention. The context of Weber's analysis is therefore too limited.

Let us turn to a fuller discussion of the aspect which Weber emphasizes—religious influence upon the intensity of the drive for profit. We should be clear that my argument is not about whether intensity of effort can vary for social reasons. I have no doubt that productive effort does vary between individuals and nations, and between different ages in the same nation. Further, I accept that this is probably determined by social environment and community attitudes. I do not question the social influence of religion in medieval and early modern times. The query I raise is whether religion was mainly an initiator of the social pressures which concern us, or whether it was mainly a (powerful) medium through which these pressures were applied. Note that if it was a medium of communication it may still have had an important sifting and modifying role of its own—shaping the pressures for change into a mould consistent with 'basic' religious precepts.

Religious leaders may simply have picked up changing community opinion and realistically accommodated to these changes though working to mould them, much as a statesman discerns changing ideas of the

[32] Max Weber, 1930, pp. 73–4.

electorate but shapes his legislative reaction according to his own views and preconceptions. But of course a statesman may do more than simply give his own bias to community demands: occasionally he plays the part of true leader, educating the electorate to accept a new idea. Thus as a leader, a statesman may play two different roles. He may be a leader because he is the first to discern a new trend in the community. By careful analysis and teaching he will come to convince the electorate that their situation has altered and that appropriate action is necessary. Alternatively, he may try to lead the electorate in an entirely new direction simply on the basis of his own convictions or ideas—he becomes a pathbreaker. Weber's idea of the part played by the Protestant ethic is analogous to the latter. He certainly does not believe that it was only discernment of a new situation which made religion a leader. The leadership was pathbreaking and conceptual (though the full implications of the concepts were unforeseen). It was derived from the Reformation: it did not simply tolerate a new situation, and did not grow out of material conditions.

Is Weber right? Was it a theological force which was an independent stimulus to the growth of capitalism? Or is it more likely that religious attitudes towards business changed as the economic situation changed? In fairness we must note that, although Weber's thesis is not a social approval thesis, it is not possible to reverse this statement to say that Weber denies the possibility that social approval played a part. Indeed, certain of Weber's statements give a hint of social approval: 'the influence of Calvinism was exerted more in the direction of the liberation of energy for private acquisition.'[33] Nevertheless, the implication is that social approval was much less significant than the positive influences of the Protestant ethic. In this I believe Weber was mistaken. An alternative interpretation sees the improving social position of businessmen, liberalized attitudes towards business practices, and a growing emphasis upon material reward as all forming a part of the one process. They were all the outcome of economic growth which changed the social position of businessmen. From being parasites greedily taking advantage of men's weaknesses, businessmen were gradually recognized as creators of opportunity and wealth, as they put men in touch with new products and with new and expanding markets.

Changing attitudes to wealth and business may in turn stimulate the drive to attain it. Status in a stagnant society is typically determined by class or caste; wealth will be sought mainly to satisfy consumption wants. In a society where wealth can purchase status more readily a new dimension will be added. Wealth accumulation now becomes a means of social mobility as well as a consumption satisfier. Hence the

[33] Max Weber, 1930, p. 151.

search for wealth is likely to become much more intense than it would be if wealth were unable to improve social position.

An expanding economy, more tolerant attitudes towards wealth accumulation, and growing social significance of wealth are likely to go together and to stimulate the intensity of wealth seeking. This, in turn, may further stimulate economic growth—and so on: the process may be cumulative and the components mutually interacting.

A social approval thesis seems to fit the facts much more satisfactorily, particularly applied to Europe as a whole. A social approval thesis is more consistent with a Europe where religion was losing its importance at the same time as capitalism was on the ascendancy. It is more consistent with the marked differences in capitalistic tendencies between Protestant sects in different circumstances, and with the capitalistic achievements in Catholic communities such as Belgium. It is a thesis which emphasizes graduations in the influence of new ideas. It is easier to reconcile with a two-way mutual interaction between attitudes and economic change. It also has the virtue of going some way towards explaining the disagreements between modern scholars. Yet it does not deny the possibility that Protestants led the way, nor the possibility that there were positive aspects of Protestants' attitudes; nor yet does it deny the possibility that religious changes were very real and important determinants of the rate of economic growth—by influencing the pace of change in community attitudes.

The fact that changes in economic attitudes seem to have a universal flavour in Western Europe suggests that some more universal force than the Protestant ethic was at work. Samuelsson sees little substantial difference between Catholic and Protestant attitudes towards economic matters, though even he seems to admit *some* correlation between economic and religious progressiveness.[34] Such a correlation is to be expected on general grounds. The newer churches, whose very existence was based on rethinking of old doctrines, would be more likely both to accept new economic doctrines and to attract those whose economic attitudes were 'advanced'. However we cannot avoid the undoubted fact that the Catholic Church was changing too, as can be seen in the remarkable rise in the strength of the pragmatic Jesuits, or in the industrialization of Catholic Belgium not long after England. If changes in religious attitudes towards economic matters were seen principally as responses to changing economic circumstance, this would explain the universal element in changing attitudes, and can also incorporate the more ready response of the Protestants. On the other hand, the Weber thesis cannot explain the universal element.

A social approval thesis also more easily explains why there were

[34] K. Samuelsson, 1961, pp. 27–8, 102.

more or less simultaneous changes in attitudes towards money-making, towards certain occupations, and towards some business practices such as interest-taking and competitive pricing. Weber's thesis only explains the first of these. There seems no logical reason why the idea of daily hard work in the service of God should have produced changes in the status of some occupations or have made Protestants more tolerant of usury. Under the Weber thesis the coincidence of these various changes is therefore somewhat mysterious.

Again, the Weber thesis has some difficulty in explaining why the most far-reaching consequences of the ethic was so long delayed after the Reformation. Tawney agrees that its greatest influence was delayed.[35] If it was really the Protestant ethic which transformed man's economic life, why was the transformation so long delayed? Weber is vague on this point. Tawney argues that the liberating attributes of the new doctrines only became effective in a suitable environment. In England, that environment did not emerge until after the Civil War.[36] It was only then that the nascent individualism of the Protestant ethic emerged and religion abdicated 'its theoretical primacy over economic activity and social institutions'.[37] The rise of individualism had been stoutly resisted by the divines. It was only when individualism at last gained the ascendancy that it combined with religious duty[38] (calling) to produce an economic revolution in which 'the conscientious discharge of the duties of business, is among the loftiest of religious and moral virtues'.[39]

It is curious that the impact of the idea of calling was so delayed. The idea was not a nascent or hidden aspect of Protestant doctrine which only gradually emerged. Did it, like individualism, require a favourable environment to be effective? And if the concept was theologically based, why did it exercise its greatest influence on Protestants after the iron discipline of the Protestants had broken down?[40]

Similarly, it is odd that the ethic should be said to be exerting its greatest influence at the very time when European life was becoming secularized. We are told that when religion was losing its overwhelming influence upon daily life, it was imparting a new kind of impulse to the community which was pervasive and revolutionary in its impact. We are invited to believe in a kind of drones' flight. A more plausible assumption is that the changing economic situation invited both a response from the religious bodies and a retreat from religion, as men came to see other bases to their lives.

[35] R. H. Tawney, 2nd edn. 1937, pp. 84–5, 226–7, 232.
[36] *Ibid.*
[37] *Ibid.*, p. 84.
[38] *Ibid.*, p. 240.
[39] *Ibid.*, p. 241.
[40] See footnote 35 above, also p. 213.

Further, in so far as the writings of the great leaders are at all useful, they indicate that men were struggling with a great moral dilemma at this time. Wesley condemned slothfulness and said that each man should work assiduously at his daily task, but he was well aware that this was at variance with the idea that wealth was dangerous and the pursuit of wealth perfidious. Wesley's solution to the dilemma was an uneasy compromise—one should give away the extra fruits of one's labour.[41] This curious mixture of old and new moral attitudes is probably indicative of the very real dilemma which faced the moralist of the early modern period, unwilling to abandon the old concepts which viewed the craving for wealth as morally debilitating, yet no longer bound by the economic reality which made such a doctrine socially necessary in the comparative economic stagnation of the Middle Ages.

The dilemma was reflected above all in the increasing emphasis upon the rule of conscience in economic matters. This was a reflection of the growing impossibility of laying down strict rules of economic conduct in a changing and buoyant economic world. The spread of the rule of conscience is one indication of moral uncertainity, and it is also a reflection of the basis of that uncertainity—the change in economic circumstances. It was no longer possible to condemn out of hand some economic practices, such as the taking of interest. Calvin understood this. Nor was the rapid accumulation of wealth to be condemned unequivocally, as it could in an age of economic stagnation when rapid gathering of wealth by one man would normally be at the expense of others. An ethic of rigid wealth-sharing is a bolster to the necessary institutional arrangements for a stable society in a stagnant economy. But such attitudes are placed under pressure in an expanding economy where the *nouveaux riches* are not necessarily depriving others, and indeed may even be providing work and income for others. If, however, the accumulation of wealth was not wrong *per se*, it was still wrong to crush others on your way to wealth and to covet wealth for its own sake. Here, then, was the dilemma of the moralists which they resolved by emphasis on the *motives* for action: upon conscience. In medieval times specific exceptions had been made to the rule about wealth accumulation, but as Western Europe expanded economically such a system became unworkable in general, and so the moralist had to place the responsibility for judgement upon the individual and his conscience, and in doing so opened the way for moral flexibility.

At a more specific level Samuelsson argues that the Protestant sects accommodated themselves to the needs of their flocks.[42] This is not to imply any base motives on their part. It may be seen simply as a

---

[41] See notes 5, 6, and 7 above.
[42] K. Samuelsson, 1961, Ch. 2; also W. J. Warner, 1967, pp. 200–6.

recognition of changing circumstances. Indeed, the recognition probably lagged well behind the reality: men are accustomed to regard their ethical systems as immutable and independent of practical matters, though of course they are not. Hence the tendency was probably towards perpetuating an ethical system which Western Europe had outgrown, rather than the reverse.

However, the pressures for change were not uniform throughout Europe, and the process was long and agonizing. This perhaps explains why countries such as Spain, which had experienced a short flush of economic expansion, could finish at the rear of the changes in ethical standards. (In Spain also, the treasures of the sixteenth century may have been reserved by a relatively small group, so that the old morality was still appropriate for the ordinary men. Something of this dichotomy must apply to most countries.)

Weber specifically denies that the ethic was the outcome of economic change,[43] arguing that the capitalistic spirit was manifest in economically primitive America in the eighteenth century. However, it is not the stage of development of the economy that matters, but whether it is expansionist or stagnant; and America was growing even more rapidly than Britain in the eighteenth century, if population growth is any indication.

If this is similar to H. M. Robertson's view,[44] it differs from Robertson in that I still emphasize religion as a vital determinant of economic progress in the early modern period, as a consequence of a mutual interaction between the economy and religious ideas. Any ethical or value system must influence economic efficiency, by prescribing methods and determining motives and ambitions. Religion continued to dominate European value systems in the early modern period and hence was still a major influence upon economic action. Consequently the pace of religious rethinking of economic issues must have been a prime determinant of the pace of economic progress. Robertson would possibly agree that mutual interaction was involved—it is implicit in some of his analysis—but I emphasize it explicitly. The speed of change in attitudes towards business must have influenced economic progress, and this remains true no matter where one discerns the origins of religious change.

Nevertheless, the Reformation was perhaps the result of a general social upheaval to which economic changes formed the background. It may be significant, for instance, that Calvin lived in Switzerland, closely associated with the economic progress of the northern Italian city states; but it is not necessary to see such a direct and exclusive

[43] See note 15 above.
[44] H. M. Robertson, 1959.

relationship. Perhaps Protestantism can be seen as a spiritualistic formulation of the ideas of individualism. Those who were moving intellectually towards individualism would probably be inclined to adopt Protestantism, which was perhaps a branch of the individualistic movement. There was a strong connection between the spread of individualistic thinking and economic change, because it was economic change which made individualism practical and perhaps feasible for a growing number of men. Individualism gathered strength as it became relevant to more and more men, and so did Protestantism. In turn, the spiritual sanction Protestantism gave to individualism hastened and strengthened the movement towards the latter.

It is also possible to argue that the Reformation rested less on the individual leader than on the recognition by ordinary people that the old ways were no longer appropriate. Even if Luther was not conscious of a changing world around him, the responsive chord which he struck may have been heard because of such awareness. In other words the question may be not why Luther (or Calvin) did what he did, and said what he did, but why people followed him and continued to follow him. After all, there had been reformers in the past who had sometimes been absorbed by the Church and sometimes successfully resisted. Individuals had experienced moments of glory, only to be crushed by their own followers who came to recognize the dangers of the new doctrine.

All this is not to deny that the Reformation and the Protestant ethic may have had positive aspects—in particular what Peacock[45] calls goal-oriented action rather than harmony-oriented action, or what McClelland[46] calls high achievement motivation. Nor does it deny that the *conscious* use of religious power or ideology can profoundly influence economic performance.[47] Nevertheless, in the context we are examining it is impossible to ignore the importance of the gradual response of attitudes to changing circumstance, and it is difficult to see the positive aspects outweighing the social approval aspects of religious change. Further, in the framework of response, some people and communities will respond more suitably than others, and will, during the process of change, take on characteristics more conducive to capitalism. This implies no more than that the response is not deterministic: it can be influenced by events, individuals and local institutions.

No matter what view we take of the relationship between the Reformation and the rise of capitalism, we would expect a relationship between social attitudes and the working of the economy—one which, I argue, worked in two directions. It is clear that medieval religious attitudes

[45] J. L. Peacock, 1969, pp. 38–40.
[46] D. C. McClelland, 1961.
[47] N. M. Hansen, 1963, pp. 462–74.

gave an ethical backing to a basically rural and stagnant economy and social system. The attitudes of an industrialized country, such as Britain had become by the mid-nineteenth century, were necessarily different. In the transition, changing economic circumstances would obviously put pressure upon the ethical system. The speed at which attitudes alter under this pressure surely reacted back upon the rate of economic growth. Hence even if the ethical changes are seen entirely as responses, they may nevertheless be a major determinant of economic progress—by limiting the classes from which entrepreneurs can be readily drawn, or limiting the kind of activities which the community sees as legitimate and socially acceptable.

FURTHER READING

BOULDING, M.: 'Religious Foundations of Economic Progress'.

ELLIOTT, C. M.: 'The Ideology of Economic Growth: A Case Study'.

HANSEN, N. M.: 'The Protestant Ethic as a General Precondition for Economic Development'.

HILL, CHRISTOPHER: 'Protestantism and the Rise of Capitalism'.
   Society and Puritanism in Pre-Revolutionary England.

MCCLELLAND, D. C. and WINTER, D. G.: *Motivating Economic Growth.*

MYA MAUNG: 'Cultural Values and Economic Change in Burma'.

PEACOCK, J. L.: 'Religion, Communications, and Modernization: A Weberian Critique of Some Recent Views'.

POLLARD, S.: *The Idea of Progress: History and Society.*

ROBERTSON, H. M.: *Aspects of the Rise of Economic Individualism.*

SAMUELSSON, K.: *Religion and Economic Action.*

SINGER, M.: 'Religion and Social Change in India: The Max Weber Thesis, Phase Three'.

TAWNEY, R. H.: *Religion and the Rise of Capitalism.*

TREVOR-ROPER, H.: *Religion, the Reformation and Social Change: and other Essays.*

WEBER, MAX: *The Protestant Ethic and the Spirit of Capitalism.*

9 Summary and Conclusion

A major aim of this thesis is to argue that economic history has great potential for studying the complex problems of industrialization which so press upon the modern world. The study of past industrializations is a vital method of understanding the process. Economic history, however, has failed to provide this understanding, and I have argued that this failure is the result of three major weaknesses in the methods and the objectives of economic historians. Let us examine each of these weaknesses in turn.

CHRONOLOGY

My emphasis on the chronological weakness of industrial revolution studies arises partly from my belief that chronology is an underrated aid to historical explanation. Chronology helps to relate a number of disparate changes to one another in some consistent way. As I have argued at some length in the first chapter, the numerous factors involved can be interrelated by employing comparative chronology or what I have called a time-chart approach.

The neglect of chronology has led to some poor history, and this remains true whether the time-chart approach to industrialization is accepted or not. Talented historians have laboriously developed ingenious explanations of historical 'phases' without establishing that the phases are legitimate. For example, we find some close analysis of the consequences of improved farming on light soils in the late seventeenth century when the very existence of widespread improvement at this time must be regarded as unproven.

The neglect of chronology is seen most obviously in agricultural history, and much of the third chapter is devoted to examining the reasons for that weakness. A similar weakness is also seen in some aspects of the population-demand relationship, in particular in the massive gap in our knowledge of when the lower classes entered the commercial markets for industrial goods.

The chronological weaknesses in entrepreneurial studies are weaknesses in exploring the dynamics of the emergence of entrepreneurial talent and initiative, and of a favourable economic environment. In capital studies there is a weakness in the study of the evolution of different types of capital source for different types of economic need at various stages of the transition to industrialization. These are weaknesses of omission rather than commission.

In fields such as the relation of modern science to British economic growth, scholarship is not sufficiently advanced for one to criticize the neglect of chronology. Few have tried to explore the relationship between intellectual and economic history. When historians come to do so, the timing of intellectual developments will obviously be of prime importance.

It should be emphasized that the weakness of chronological treatment often takes the form of imprecisely delineating phases of growth. Again this is most obviously true of agricultural history. Centuries of agrarian progress and changing technique can be traced: consequently the historian's true task is to distinguish comparative rates of change in various eras. Thus the neglect of chronology is a failure to quantify, in what is inescapably a problem of comparative quantities and rates of growth.

INTERACTIONS

The efforts of historians to deal with the interrelations in the growth process are also inadequate. They fail to understand that in the long run interrelationships are frequently, perhaps mostly, of a two-way kind—they are *mutual* interactions. The failure to grasp this underlies the kind of methodology which asks whether entrepreneurship was a cause of the industrial revolution. With the question phrased in this way we can answer 'yes' with firm historical conviction. Entrepreneurship was a cause in the sense that the superior performance of British industry over, say, French industry in the eighteenth century was undoubtedly due to the fact that the British were more dynamic than the French in using new techniques which were available to both nations. While this answer is sound enough, the question is not. It is a one-sided question which fails to recognize that British entrepreneurs may have remained superior to French over a long period because they operated in a more dynamic economy, and in a more favourable business, political and cultural environment. British entrepreneurship, British economic performance and the British social and institutional environment interacted on each other in a complex way during the long transition to industrialization. To understand this is to understand how superficial many of our research hypotheses really are.

Those scholars who have explored relationships between variables have almost invariably based their work on assumptions which ignore the importance of mutual interaction. For instance, efforts to explore the relationship between the upsurge of population and economic growth have been mostly an attempt to establish chronological primacy, on an assumption that this distinguishes cause from effect. But once again this assumption fails to recognize long-term mutual interaction.

Once we acknowledge the importance of mutual interaction we will realize that it implies a modification of the techniques and the objectives of our research. It is clear that during transition from a traditional to an industrial society a number of factors must give ground or respond in the face of change. It is also clear that the pace or depth of these responses is vital, and that this is as much a function of the conditions in which the change occurred as it is a function of the strength of the inducement to change. This is saying no more than that a given market opportunity will not find identical reactions from all men in all situations. Furthermore, future market opportunity, as men perceive it, is a function of the speed with which previous opportunities are grasped. Man's perception of opportunity is largely shaped by past experience.

These considerations may mean that it is best to avoid the words 'cause' and 'effect', if only because in the long run there are rarely clear-cut superordinate-subordinate relationships in industrialization. Thus a statement that the inventions in eighteenth-century Britain were caused by market opportunities will mislead those who take this to mean that the market growth was a sufficient condition for the inventions. No doubt market growth was a necessary condition for continuing commercial invention, but the inventions also closely depended upon a capacity to invent, and to build and to operate new equipment. This cannot be explained only in terms of short-term market opportunity.

Moreover, even if a stimulus response situation were clearly demonstrated this would only be a short-term relationship. This would be a tiny segment of the transformation process, and in the long run most such relationships would give way to a complex mutual causation pattern. This point of view underlies various parts of most chapters of this book, but it is perhaps most fully illustrated in the discussion of the roles of foreign trade and science.

In writing about foreign trade I emphasized the dangers of selecting one side or the other of the Atlantic partnership as the prime mover in trade expansion. Trade could hardly have expanded strongly without continual adjustments on both sides of the Atlantic. The ever-expanding frontiers in the Americas, the growth of population, the continuing spirit of enterprise and the commercialism of economic life, were all essential to the expansion of trade and to the switch to cotton production towards the end of the eighteenth century. Britain's main contribution to the expansion was her growing capacity to manufacture products at competitive prices. This capacity in itself, of course, is only explicable in terms of a complex process of action and reaction between a number of things: agriculture, entrepreneurship, invention, innovation, relocation of industry etc.—in short, the history of Britain's internal economic responses throughout the eighteenth century.

Any attempt to demonstrate the primacy of one side or the other is likely to obscure the truth: that in the long run the two-way relationship was paramount. Berrill, Davis, Habakkuk, Deane and Cole, in mooting one side or the other as the prime mover, have misled us by leading us away from the one fact of over-riding importance. The two sides of the Atlantic trade complemented each other, and the continuing growth of each could hardly have been possible at the same rate without the continuing growth of both.

Perhaps the major contributions of modern science was to train men's minds to a new method of analysis and problem-solving. Such training would only gradually have penetrated the various levels of society, and must have done so primarily because there was a progressive need for the kind of intellectual qualities found in modern scientific analysis. That is to say that scientific modes of thought progressively penetrated society as the increasingly technical society required the problem-solving abilities which scientific analytical techniques could bestow. In turn, the growing realization of the importance of science and of the contribution it could make to men's diagnostic skills must have stimulated science. Science contributed to men's capacity to solve their problems and in doing so it rose to a new prestige and influence as that contribution was appreciated.

THE SOCIAL BACKGROUND TO INDUSTRIALIZATION

It may be argued that almost every economic change associated with the industrial revolution had some social or cultural change as a background. No doubt the importance of the background varies from topic to topic, but I believe social and cultural influences to be grossly under-rated in modern scholarship. Perhaps the most significant impact of these influences was on the *pace* of change.

Each chapter has something to say about the influence of social and cultural factors, though the treatment varies from a few lines in some chapters to the greater part of chapters 7 and 8. This does not necessarily reflect the relative importance I attach to each. Thus, for example, it seems to me that in many parts of Asia the weight of tradition in village society is the central problem of agricultural reform, whereas it seems certain that the social barriers to agrarian change were not so significant in eighteenth-century Britain (but it is still important to understand why this was so). As the British medieval village was perhaps as antipathetic to change as is an Asian traditional village, it is important to trace the evolution from this position to that of the late eighteenth century. By this time commercial attitudes had deeply penetrated the British agrarian scene. The history of this penetration will be, I feel sure, an important part of an explanation of British growth.

This point can be generalized: even if research could demonstrate that a particular factor, such as trade expansion in the eighteenth century, was not inhibited by social obstacles it may be important to ask why they *did not* inhibit. Thus the expansion of trade depended very much on the commercial, specialist and capitalist character of American agriculturalists. What were the origins of these characteristics? Again, religious and ethical strictures may have been less inhibitive in the eighteenth century than they were in the Middle Ages. Why? British technical and problem-solving abilities seemed adequate to the needs of British industry in the eighteenth century. How did they come to be adequate? Workmen were on the whole prepared to accept labour-saving machinery, and entrepreneurs to risk their introduction. What explains these attitudes?

I strongly believe that unless these and similar questions become significant research problems, we can hardly pretend to be working towards an explanation of how and why Britain was able to achieve an industrial revolution.

Appendix

Bank Credit Creation and 'Capital Stock' in Eighteenth and Nineteenth-Century Britain

	Capital stock		Deposits and note issue[7]	Bank credit creation[8]	Increases		
	A including land[1]	B excluding land			Capital Stock A	B	Bank credit creation
1688	364[3]	112[2]	—	—			
					1096	628	34
1800	1460[4]	740[4]	43	34			
					357	177	20
1812	1817[4]	917[4]	68	54			
					601	301	19
1833	2418[4]	1218[4]	91	73			
					6022	5682	476
1885	8440[6]	6900[5]	674	549			
					—	4000	481
1913	—	10900[5]	1287	1030			

N.B. All figures are for Great Britain and represent £000,000.

[1] The question of whether to include land is of some significance. As Deane and Cole point out (Phyllis Deane and W. A. Cole, 1962, p. 272), in the eighteenth and early nineteenth century there is some justification for considering land, as the increase in value may be due to enclosure and improvements. The inclusion of land makes very little difference to the calculations after 1833.

[2] Phyllis Deane and W. A. Cole 1962, p. 260.

[3] Adding King's value of land to Deane and Cole's estimate.
Gregory King, 'Natural and Political Observations and Conclusions upon the State and Condition of England' 'Of the Naval Trade of England 1688 and the National Profit then arising thereby', both published in *Two Tracts by Gregory King*, ed. G. Barnett, The Johns Hopkins Press, Baltimore, 1936.

[4] From the estimates of Beeke, Colquhoun and Pebrer, taken from R. Giffen, *The Growth of Capital* (Bell & Sons, London, 1889), pp. 95, 103, 107.

[5] Phyllis Deane and W. A. Cole, 1962, p. 274.

[6] Adding Giffen's land valuations to Deane and Cole's calculation—Giffen, *op. cit.*, pp. 163-4.

[7] From A. Feaveryear, *The Pound Sterling* (2nd edn.), revised by E. V. Morgan (Clarendon Press, Oxford, 1963), p. 304; and Savings Bank deposits from B. R. Mitchell and Phyllis Deane, 1962, pp. 453-4. The figures are compiled on the assumption that movements between Feaveryear's reporting years change with equal yearly gradations.

[8] Deposits and note issue, less 20 per cent cash reserve ratio.

Select Bibliography

Abbreviations:

A.E.R.—American Economic Review
Agric. Hist.—Agricultural History
A.H.R.—Agricultural History Review
C.J.E.P.—Canadian Journal of Economics and Political Science
E.D.C.C.—Economic Development and Cultural Change
E.E.H.—Explorations in Entrepreneurial History
E.H.—Economic History
E.H.R.—Economic History Review
E.H.R. (2)—Economic History Review 2nd series
E. J.—Economic Journal
H.O.—Human Organization
J.E.H.—Journal of Economic History

AITKEN, HUGH (ed.) 1965: *Explorations in Enterprise*. Harvard University Press, Cambridge, Mass.

AKHLAQUR, RAHMAN M. 1963: 'Foreign Trade and the Growth of Cotton Textiles Industry in Britain'. *Pakistan Economic Journal* XIII.

ANDERSON, B. L. 1970: 'Money and the Structure of Credit in the Eighteenth Century'. *Business History* XII.

ANDERSON, C. A. and BOWMAN, M. J. (eds.) 1965: *Education and Economic Development*. Aldine, Chicago.

ARGYLE, M. 1967: 'The Social Psychology of Social Change', in T. Burns and S. B. Saul (eds.): *Social Theory and Economic Change*. Tavistock Publications, London.

ARMYTAGE, W. H. G. 1970: *Four Hundred Years of English Education* (2nd edn.). Cambridge University Press, Cambridge.

ASHTON, R. 1964–5: 'Puritanism and Progress'. *E.H.R. (2)* XVII.

ASHTON, T. S. 1949: 'Standard of Life of the Workers in England 1790–1830'. *J.E.H.* Supplement IX; reprinted in F. A. Hayek (ed.) 1954: *Capitalism and the Historians*. Routledge and Kegan Paul, London.

    1955: *An Economic History of England: The Eighteenth Century*. Methuen, London.

1959: *Economic Fluctuations in England 1700–1800*. Clarendon Press, Oxford.

1963: *Iron and Steel in the Industrial Revolution* (3rd edn.). Manchester University Press, Manchester.

1968: *The Industrial Revolution 1760–1830* (rev'd edn.). Oxford University Press, London.

ASHTON, T. S. and SAYERS, R. S. 1953: *Papers in English Monetary History*. Oxford University Press, London.

ASHTON, T. S. and SYKES, J. 1964: *The Coal Industry of the Eighteenth Century* (2nd edn.). Manchester University Press, Manchester.

AYAL, E. B. 1963: 'Value Systems and Economic Development in Japan and Thailand'. *Journal of Social Issues* XIX.

BAINES, SIR EDWARD, 1966: *History of the Cotton Manufacture in Great Britain* (2nd edn.). Frank Cass, London.

BARAN, P. A. and HOBSBAWM, E. J. 1961: 'The Stages of Economic Growth'. *Kyklos* XIV.

BARBOUR, V. 1930: 'Dutch and English Merchant Shipping in the Seventeenth Century'. *E.H.R.* II.

BARKER, T. C. 1960: 'The Beginnings of the Canal Age in the British Isles', in L. S. Pressnell (ed.): *Studies in the Industrial Revolution*. University of London Press, London.

BEALES, H. L. 1929–30: 'The Industrial Revolution'. *History* XIV.

1958: *The Industrial Revolution 1750–1850* (new edn.). Frank Cass, London.

BEER, J. 1960: 'Eighteenth-Century Theories on the Process of Dyeing'. *Isis* LI.

BENNETT, M. K. 1935: 'British Wheat Yields per acre for Seven Centuries'. *E.H.* III.

BERESFORD, M. 1961: 'Habitation versus Improvement: The Debate on Enclosure by Agreement', in F. J. Fisher (ed.): *Essays in the Economic and Social History of Tudor and Stuart England*. Cambridge University Press, Cambridge.

BERNAL, J. D. 1953: *Science and Industry in the Nineteenth Century*. Routledge and Kegan Paul, London.

1954: *Science in History*. Watts, London.

BERREMAN, G. D. 1963: 'Caste and Community Development'. *H.O.* XXII.

BERRILL, K. 1959–60: 'International Trade and the Rate of Economic Growth'. *E.H.R.* (2) XII.

BOSERUP, ESTER, 1965: *The Conditions of Agricultural Growth: The Economics of Agrarian Change under Population Pressure*. Allen and Unwin, London.

BOULDING, K. 1952: 'Religious Foundations of Economic Progress'. *Harvard Business Review* XXX.

BRADBURN, NORMAN N. and BERLEW, DAVID E. 1961–2: 'Need for Achievement and English Industrial Growth'. *E.D.C.C.* X.

BRENNER, Y. S. 1961–2: 'The Inflation of Prices in Early Sixteenth Century England'. *E.H.R.* (2) XIV.
  1962–3: 'The Inflation of Prices in England, 1551–1650'. *E.H.R.* (2) XV.

BRONOWSKI, J. and MAZLISH, B. 1960: *The Western Intellectual Tradition: From Leonardo to Hegel.* Hutchinson, London.

BRYSON, G. 1968: *Man and Society: The Scottish Inquiry of the Eighteenth Century.* Kelley, New York.

BUER, M. C. 1926: *Health, Wealth, and Population in the Early Days of the Industrial Revolution.* Routledge, London.

BURNETT, JOHN, 1966: *Plenty and Want: A Social History of Diet in England from 1815 to the Present Day.* Nelson, London.

BUTTERFIELD, H. 1959: 'The History of Science and the Study of History'. *Harvard Library Bulletin* XIII.

CAIRNCROSS, A. K. 1960: 'International Trade and Economic Development'. *Kyklos* XIII.
  1960–61: 'The Stages of Economic Growth'. *E.H.R.* (2) XIII.
  1962: *Factors in Economic Development.* Allen and Unwin, London.

CAMERON, RONDO *et al.* 1967: *Banking in the Early Stages of Industrialization: A Study in Comparative Economic History.* Oxford University Press, New York.

CARDWELL, D. S. L. 1957: *The Organization of Science in England.* Heinemann, London.
  1963: *Steam Power in the Eighteenth Century: A Case Study in the Application of Science.* Sheed and Ward, London.

CHAMBERS, J. D. 1940: 'Enclosure and the Small Landowner'. *E.H.R.* X.
  1952–3: 'Enclosure and the Labour Supply in the Industrial Revolution'. *E.H.R.* (2) V.
  1957: *The Vale of Trent 1670–1800. E.H.R.* Supplement III.
  1960: 'Industrialization as a Factor in Economic Growth in England, 1700–1900', in *First International Conference of Economic History: Contributions and Communications.* Moulton, Paris.
  1961: *The Workshop of the World: British Economic History 1820–1880.* Oxford University Press, London.
  1966: *Nottinghamshire in the Eighteenth Century* (2nd edn.). Frank Cass, London.

CHAMBERS, J. D. and MINGAY, G. E. 1966: *The Agricultural Revolution 1750–1880.* Batsford, London.

CHAPMAN, S. D. 1965: 'The Transition to the Factory System in the Midlands Cotton-Spinning Industry'. *E.H.R.* (*2*) XVIII.

1967: *The Early Factory Masters: The Transition to the Factory System in the Midland Textile Industry*. David and Charles, Newton Abbot.

1970: 'Fixed Capital Formation in the British Cotton Industry, 1770–1815'. *E.H.R.* (*2*) XXIII.

CLAPHAM, J. H. 1923: 'The Growth of an Agrarian Proletariat 1688–1832'. *Cambridge Historical Journal* I.

1930–38: *Economic History of Modern Britain* (3 vols.). Cambridge University Press, Cambridge.

1936: *The Economic Development of France and Germany 1815–1914* (4th edn.). Cambridge University Press, Cambridge.

1944: *The Bank of England* (2 vols.). Cambridge University Press, Cambridge.

1957: *A Concise Economic History of Britain to 1750*. Cambridge University Press, Cambridge.

CLARK, G. N. 1923: 'The Navigation Act of 1651'. *History* New Series, VII.

1937: *Science and Social Welfare in the Age of Newton*. Oxford University Press, London.

1938: *Guide to English Commercial Statistics 1696–1782*. Royal Historical Society, London.

1953: *The Idea of the Industrial Revolution*. David Murray Memorial Lecture, Jackson, Glasgow.

CLAY, C. 1968: 'Marriage, Inheritance, and the Rise of the Large Estates in England, 1660–1815'. *E.H.R.* (*2*) XXI.

CLOW, A. and CLOW, N. 1952: *The Chemical Revolution*. Batchworth, London.

1956: 'The Timber Famine and the Development of Technology'. *Annals of Science* XII.

COATS, A. W. 1956–7: 'Changing Attitudes to Labour in the Mid-Eighteenth Century'. *E.H.R.* (*2*) XI.

COCHRANE, R. C. 1956: 'Francis Bacon and the Rise of the Mechanical Arts in Eighteenth-Century England'. *Annals of Science* XII.

COLE, W. A. 1957–8: 'Trends in Eighteenth-Century Smuggling'. *E.H.R.* (*2*) X.

1958–9: 'The Measurement of Industrial Growth'. *E.H.R.* (*2*) XI.

COLEMAN, D. C. 1955–6: 'Labour in the English Economy of the Seventeenth Century'. *E.H.R.* (*2*) VIII.

1956: 'Industrial Growth and Industrial Revolutions'. *Economica* New Series, XXIII; reprinted in E. M. Carus-Wilson (ed.) 1962: *Essays in Economic History*, (Vol. 3). Edward Arnold, London.

COTGROVE, S. E. 1958: *Technical Education and Social Change*. Allen and Unwin, London.

COURT, W. H. B. 1954: *A Concise Economic History of Britain from 1750 to Recent Times*. Cambridge University Press, Cambridge.

CROMBIE, A. C. 1952: *Augustine to Galileo: The History of Science A.D. 400–1650*. Falcon Press, London.

1953: *Robert Grosseteste and the Origins of Experimental Science, 1100–1700*. Clarendon Press, Oxford.

1960: 'Historians and the Scientific Revolution'. *Endeavour* XIX.

1963: *Scientific Change*. Heinemann, London.

CROWTHER, J. G. 1962: *Scientists of the Industrial Revolution*. The Cresset Press, London.

DAVIES, E. 1927–8: 'The Small Landowner, 1780–1832, in the Light of Land Tax Assessments'. *E.H.R.* I.

DAVIES, K. G. 1960–61: 'Empire and Capital'. *E.H.R.* (2) XIII.

DAVIS, R. 1954–5: 'English Foreign Trade 1660–1700'. *E.H.R.* (2) VII.

1962–3: 'English Foreign Trade 1700–1774'. *E.H.R.* (2) XV.

DEANE, PHYLLIS, 1955–6a: 'Contemporary Estimates of National Income in the First Half of the Nineteenth Century'. *E.H.R.* (2) VIII.

1955–6b: 'The Implications of Early National Income Estimates for the Measurement of Long-Term Economic Growth in the United Kingdom'. *E.D.C.C.* IV.

1956-7: 'The Industrial Revolution and Economic Growth: The Evidence of Early British National Income Estimates'. *E.D.C.C.* V.

1957: 'The Output of the British Woolen Industry in the Eighteenth Century'. *J.E.H.* XVII.

1960–1: 'Capital Formation in Britain before the Railway Age'. *E.D.C.C.* IX.

1961: 'Long-Term Trends in World Economic Growth'. *Malayan Economic Review* VI.

1965: *The First Industrial Revolution*. Cambridge University Press, Cambridge.

DEANE, PHYLLIS and COLE, W. A. 1962: *British Economic Growth 1688–1959*. Cambridge University Press, Cambridge.

DEWEY, J. 1909: *How We Think*. Heath, London.

DICKSON, P. G. N. 1967: *The Financial Revolution in England*. Macmillan, London.

DOBB, M. 1964: 'Prelude to the Industrial Revolution'. *Science and Society* XXVIII.

DOMAR, E. D. 1961: 'On the Measurement of Technological Change'. *E.J.* LXXI.

DORE, RONALD, 1960: 'Agricultural Improvement in Japan 1870–1900'. *E.D.C.C.* IX.

DRAKE, M. (ed.) 1969: *Population in Industrialization*. Methuen, London.

DRUMMOND, J. C. and WILBRAHAM, A. 1957: *The Englishman's Food: A History of Five Centuries of English Diet* (rev'd edn.). Jonathan Cape, London.

EASTERLIN, R. A. 1965: 'Is there a need for historical research on under-development?' *A.E.R. Papers and Proceedings* LV.

ELLIOTT, C. M. 1967: 'The Ideology of Economic Growth: A Case Study', in E. L. Jones and G. E. Mingay (eds.): *Land, Labour and Population in the Industrial Revolution*. Edward Arnold, London.

ERNLE, LORD, 1961: *English Farming Past and Present* (6th edn.). Heinemann, London.

EVERSLEY, D. E. C. 1960: 'Population and Economic Growth in England before the "Take-Off"'. *International Conference of Economic History, Stockholm, 1960—Contributions and Communications*. Mouton, The Hague.

— 1967: 'The Home Market and Economic Growth in England, 1750–80', in E. L. Jones and G. E. Mingay (eds.): *Land, Labour and Population in the Industrial Revolution*. Edward Arnold, London.

FARNIE, D. A. 1962–3: 'The Commercial Empire of the Atlantic, 1607–1783'. *E.H.R.* (2) XV.

FEAVERYEAR, A. E. 1963: *The Pound Sterling: A History of English Money* (2nd edn. revised by E. V. Morgan). Clarendon Press, Oxford.

FIRTH, R. 1963: 'Money, Work and Social Change in Indo-Pacific Economic Systems', in J. Meynaud (ed.): *Social Change and Economic Development*. U.N.E.S.C.O., Paris.

FISHER, F. J. 1935: 'The Development of the London Food Market, 1540–1640'. *E.H.R.* V.

FISHLOW, A. 1965: 'Empty Economic Stages?' *E.J.* LXXV.

FLEMING, D. 1952: 'Latent Heat and the Invention of the Watt Engine'. *Isis* XLIII.

FLINN, M. W. 1958–9: 'The Growth of the English Iron Industry 1660–1760'. *E.H.R.* (2) XI.

— 1959: 'Timber and the Advance of Technology: A Reconsideration'. *Annals of Science* XV.

— 1962: *Men of Iron: The Crowleys in the Early Iron Industry*. Edinburgh University Press, Edinburgh.

— 1966a: 'Agricultural Productivity and Economic Growth in England 1700–1760: A Comment'. *J.E.H.* XXVI.

— 1966b: *The Origins of the Industrial Revolution*. Longmans, London.

1967: 'Social Theory and the Industrial Revolution', in T. Burns and S. B. Saul (eds.): *Social Theory and Economic Change*. Tavistock Publications, London.

1970: *British Population Growth 1700–1850*. Macmillan, London.

FRANKEL, S. H. 1963: 'Some Conceptual Aspects of Technical Change', in J. Meynaud (ed.): *Social Change and Economic Development*. U.N.E.S.C.O., Paris.

FRASER, T. M. JR. 1963: 'Sociocultural Parameters in Directed Change'. *H.O.* XXII.

FUSSELL, G. E. 1929: 'The Size of English Cattle in the Eighteenth Century'. *Agric. Hist.* III.

1959: 'Low Countries' Influence on English Farming'. *English Historical Review* LXXIV.

1966a: *The English Dairyfarmer 1500–1900*. Frank Cass, London.

1966b: *Farming Technique from Prehistory to Modern Times*. Pergamon Press, Oxford.

GEERTS, C. 1956: *The Social Context of Economic Change: An Indonesian Case Study*. Massachusetts Institute of Technology Press, Cambridge, Mass.

GEORGE, M. D. 1953: *England in Transition: Life and Work in the Eighteenth Century*. Penguin, London.

GERSCHENKRON, A. 1952: 'Economic Backwardness in Historical Perspective', in B. F. Hoselitz (ed.): *The Progress of Underdeveloped Areas*. Chicago University Press, Chicago.

1953: 'Social Attitudes, Entrepreneurship, and Economic Development'. *E.E.H.* VI; reprinted in L. Dupriez (ed.) 1955: *Economic Progress*. Institut de Recherches Economiques et Sociales, Louvain.

1954: 'Some Further Notes on Social Attitudes, Entrepreneurship, and Economic Development'. *E.E.H.* VII.

1962: *Economic Backwardness in Historical Perspective*. Harvard University Press, Cambridge, Mass.

1966: 'The Modernization of Entrepreneurship', in M. Weiner (ed.): *Modernization: The Dynamics of Growth*. Basic Books, New York.

1968: *Continuity in History and Other Essays*. Belknap Press, Cambridge, Mass.

GILBOY, E. B. 1932: 'Demand as a Factor in the Industrial Revolution', in *Facts and Factors in Economic History: Essays in Honour of E. F. Gay*. Harvard University Press, Cambridge, Mass. Reprinted in R. M. Hartwell (ed.) 1967: *Causes of the Industrial Revolution in England*. Methuen, London.

GILFILLAN, S. C. 1945: 'Invention as a Factor in Economic History'. *J.E.H.* Supplement V.

GILLESPIE, C. C. 1957: 'The Natural History of Industry'. *Isis* XLVIII.

GLASS, D. V. and EVERSLEY, D. E. C. 1965: *Population in History: Essays in Historical Demography*. Edward Arnold, London.

GOLDSCHMIDT, W. R. 1952: 'The Interrelations between Cultural Factors and the Acquisition of New Technical Skills', in B. F. Hoselitz (ed.): *The Progress of Underdeveloped Areas*. Chicago University Press, Chicago.

GOULD, J. D. 1962: 'Agricultural Fluctuations and the English Economy in the Eighteenth Century'. *J.E.H.* XXII.

1969: 'Hypothetical History'. *E.H.R.* (2) XXII.

GRANGER, C. W. J. and ELLIOTT, C. M. 1967: 'A Fresh Look at Wheat Prices and Markets in the Eighteenth Century'. *E.H.R.* (2) XX.

GRAY, H. L. 1959: *English Field Systems*. Harvard University Press, Cambridge, Mass.

GRIFFITH, G. TALBOT 1926: *Population Problems of the Age of Malthus*. Cambridge University Press, Cambridge.

HABAKKUK, H. J. 1940: 'English Land Ownership, 1680–1740'. *E.H.R.* X.

1953: 'Economic Functions of English Landowners in the Seventeenth and Eighteenth Centuries'. *E.E.H.* VI.

1953–4: 'English Population in the Eighteenth Century'. *E.H.R.* (2) VI.

1958: 'The Economic History of Modern Britain'. *J.E.H.* XVIII.

1961: 'Review of W. W. Rostow's "The Stages of Economic Growth"'. *E.J.* LXXI.

1963: 'Population Problems and European Economic Development in the Late Eighteenth and Nineteenth Centuries'. *A.E.R. Papers and Proceedings* LIII.

1965a: 'Historical Experience of Economic Development', in E. A. G. Robinson (ed.): *Problems in Economic Development*. Macmillan, London.

1965b: 'Landowners and the Civil War'. *E.H.R.* (2) XVIII.

1971: *Population Growth and Economic Development since 1750*. Leicester University Press, Leicester.

HABAKKUK, H. J. and DEANE, PHYLLIS, 1963: 'The Take-Off in Britain', in W. W. Rostow (ed.): *The Economics of Take-Off into Sustained Growth*. Macmillan, London.

HABAKKUK, H. J. and POSTAN, M. (eds.) 1965: *The Cambridge Economic History of Europe*: Vol. VI, *The Industrial Revolution and After*. Cambridge University Press, Cambridge.

HAGEN, E. 1962a: 'A Framework for Analysing Economic and Political Change', in Brookings Institution: *Development of the Emerging Countries*. Washington.

1962b: *On the Theory of Social Change: How Economic Growth Begins*. Dorsey Press, Homewood, Illinois.

1963: 'How Economic Growth Begins: A Theory of Social Change'. *Journal of Social Issues* XIX.

HALL, A. R. 1963: *From Galileo to Newton 1630–1720*. Collins, London.

HAMILTON, E. J. 1929: 'American Treasure and the Rise of Capitalism (1500–1700)'. *Economica* IX.

1941: 'Profit Inflation and the Industrial Revolution 1751–1800'. *Quarterly Journal of Economics* LVI.

HAMILTON, H. 1967: *English Brass and Copper Industries to 1800* (2nd edn.). Frank Cass, London.

HANS, N. A. 1951: *New Trends in Education in the Eighteenth Century*. Routledge & Kegan Paul, London.

HANSEN, N. M. 1963: 'The Protestant Ethic as a General Precondition for Economic Development'. *C.J.E.P.* XXIX.

HARBISON, F. H. and MYERS, C. A. 1959: *Management in the Industrial World*. McGraw-Hill, New York.

1964: *Education, Manpower and Economic Growth*. McGraw-Hill, New York.

HARTWELL, R. M. 1959: 'Interpretations of the Industrial Revolution in England: A Methodological Inquiry'. *J.E.H.* XIX.

1960–61: 'The Rising Standard of Living in England, 1800–1850'. *E.H.R.* (2) XIII.

1965a: *The Industrial Revolution in England*. Historical Association Pamphlet, General Series, No. 58.

1965b: 'The Causes of the Industrial Revolution: An Essay in Methodology'. *E.H.R.* (2) XVIII.

(ed.) 1967: *The Causes of the Industrial Revolution in England*. Methuen, London.

1969: 'Economic Growth in England before the Industrial Revolution: Some Methodological Issues'. *J.E.H.* XXIX.

(ed.) 1970: *The Industrial Revolution*. Blackwell, Oxford.

1971: *The Industrial Revolution and Economic Growth*. Methuen, London.

HAVINDEN, M. A. 1961: 'Agricultural Progress in Open-Field Oxfordshire'. *A.H.R.* IX.

HAYAMI, Y. and YAMADA, S. 1968: 'Technological Progress in Agriculture', in L. Klein and K. Ohkawa (eds.): *Economic Growth: The Japanese Experience since the Meiji Era*. Irwin, Homewood, Illinois.

HEATON, H. 1965: *The Yorkshire Woollen and Worsted Industries* (2nd edn.). Clarendon Press, Oxford.

HELLEINER, K. F. 1957: 'The Vital Revolution Reconsidered'. *C.J.E.P.* XXIII.

HENDERSON, W. O. 1965: *Britain and Industrial Europe 1750–1870* (2nd edn.). Leicester University Press, Leicester.

HIGGINS, J. P. P. and POLLARD, S. 1971: *Aspects of Capital Investment in Great Britain 1750–1850.* Methuen, London.

HILL, CHRISTOPHER 1961: 'Protestantism and the Rise of Capitalism', in F. J. Fisher (ed.): *Essays in the Economic and Social History of Tudor and Stuart England.* Cambridge University Press, Cambridge.

1964a: *Society and Puritanism in Pre-Revolutionary England.* Secker and Warburg, London.

1964b: 'William Harvey and the Idea of Monarchy'. *Past and Present* XXVII.

1967: *Reformation to Industrial Revolution: A Social and Economic History of Britain 1530–1780.* Weidenfeld and Nicolson, London.

HILLS, R. L. 1970: *Power in the Industrial Revolution.* Manchester University Press, Manchester.

HIRSCHMAN, A. O. 1961: *The Strategy of Economic Development.* Yale University Press, New Haven and London.

1965: 'Obstacles to Development: a Classification and a Quasi-Vanishing Act'. *E.D.C.C.* XIII.

HIRSCHMEIER, J. 1964: *The Origins of Entrepreneurship in Meiji Japan.* Harvard University Press, Cambridge, Mass.

HOBSBAWM, E. J. 1957–8: 'The British Standard of Living, 1790–1850'. *E.H R.* (2) X.

1964: *Labouring Men: Studies in the History of Labour.* Weidenfeld and Nicolson, London.

1968: *Industry and Empire: An Economic History of Britain Since 1750.* Weidenfeld and Nicolson, London.

HOBSBAWM, E. J. and HARTWELL, R. M. 1963–4: 'The Standard of Living during the Industrial Revolution: A Discussion'. *E.H.R.* (2) XVI.

HOFFMANN, W. G. 1955: *British Industry 1700–1950.* Blackwell, Oxford.

HOGBEN, LANCELOT, 1939: 'The Theoretical Leadership of Scottish Science in the English Industrial Revolution', in Lancelot Hogben: *Dangerous Thoughts.* Allen and Unwin, London.

HOLLINGSWORTH, T. H. 1957: 'A Demographic Study of the British Ducal Families'. *Population Studies* XI.

HORSEFIELD, J. K. 1960: *British Monetary Experiments 1650–1710.* London School of Economics and Bell, London.

HOSELITZ, B. F. 1952–3: 'Non-Economic Barriers to Economic Development'. *E.D.C.C.* I.

1955: 'Entrepreneurship and Capital Formation in France and Britain since 1700', in National Bureau of Economic Research: *Capital Formation and Economic Growth.* Princeton University Press, Princeton, New Jersey.

1957: 'Population Pressure, Industrialization and Social Mobility'. *Population Studies* XI.

1962: 'Entrepreneurship and Economic Growth'; 'Social Structure and Economic Growth'; 'A Sociological Approach to Economic Development'; in B. F. Hoselitz: *Sociological Aspects of Economic Growth*. Free Press, Glencoe.

HOSKINS, W. G. 1951: 'The Leicestershire Farmer in the Seventeenth Century'. *Agric. Hist.* XXV.

1954: 'Regional Farming in England'. *A.H.R.* II.

1955: *The Making of the English Landscape*. Hodder and Stoughton, London.

1957: *The Midland Peasant: The Economic and Social History of a Leicestershire Village*. Macmillan, London.

1968: 'Harvest Fluctuations and English Economic History, 1620–1759'. *A.H.R.* XVI.

HUGHES, J. R. T. 1964: 'Measuring British Economic Growth'. *J.E.H.* XXIV.

HUNT, H. G. 1957: 'The Chronology of Parliamentary Enclosure in Leicestershire'. *E.H.R.* (2) X.

1958–9: 'Landownership and Enclosure 1750–1830'. *E.H.R.* (2) XI.

HURST, J. S. 1971: 'Professor West on Early Nineteenth-Century Education'. *E.H.R.* (2) XXIV.

HUTT, W. H. 1954: 'The Factory System of the Early Nineteenth Century', in F. H. Hayek (ed.): *Capitalism and the Historians*. Routledge and Kegan Paul, London.

JACKMAN, W. T. 1962: *The Development of Transportation in Modern England* (2nd edn.). Frank Cass, London.

JOHN, A. H. 1950: *The Industrial Revolution of South Wales, 1750–1830*. University of Wales Press, Cardiff.

1953: 'Insurance Investment and the London Money Market of the Eighteenth Century'. *Economica* XX.

1954–5: 'War and the English Economy, 1700–1763'. *E.H.R.* (2) VII.

1961: 'Aspects of English Economic Growth in the First Half of the Eighteenth Century'. *Economica* New Series, XXVII.

1962: 'The Course of Agricultural Change 1660–1760', in L. S. Pressnell (ed.): *Studies in the Industrial Revolution*. University of London Press, London.

1965: 'Agricultural Productivity and Economic Growth in England 1700–1760'. *J.E.H.* XXV; reprinted in E. L. Jones (ed.) 1967: *Agriculture and Economic Growth in England 1650–1815*. Methuen, London.

JONES, E. L. 1960: 'Eighteenth-Century Changes in Hampshire Chalkland Farming'. *A.H.R.* VIII.

1962–3: 'English Farming before and during the Nineteenth Century'. *E.H.R.* (2) XV.

1965: 'Agricultural and Economic Growth in England 1660–1750: Agricultural Change'. *J.E.H.* XXV.

(ed.) 1967: *Agriculture and Economic Growth in England 1650–1815.* Methuen, London.

1968: 'Agricultural Origins of Industry'. *Past and Present* XL.

JOSLIN, D. M. 1954–5: 'London Private Bankers 1720–85'. *E.H.R.* (2) VII.

KERRIDGE, E. 1955–6: 'Turnip Husbandry in High Suffolk'. *E.H.R.* (2) VIII.

1967: *The Agricultural Revolution.* Allen and Unwin, London.

1969: 'The Agricultural Revolution Reconsidered'. *Agric. Hist.* XLIII.

KRAUSE, J. T. 1958–9a: 'Changes in English Fertility and Mortality 1781–1850'. *E.H.R.* (2) XI.

1958–9b: 'Some Implications of Recent Research in Historical Demography'. *Comparative Studies in Society and History* I.

1959: 'Some Neglected Factors in the English Industrial Revolution'. *J.E.H.* XIX.

1961: 'English Population Movements between 1700 and 1850'. *International Population Conference, New York*; reprinted in M. Drake (ed.) 1969: *Population in Industrialization.* Methuen, London.

KUNKEL, J. H. 1963: 'Psychological Factors in the Analysis of Economic Development'. *Journal of Social Issues* XIX.

KUZNETS, S. 1955: 'Population, Income and Capital', in L. H. Dupriez (ed.): *Economic Progress.* Institut de Recherches Economiques et Sociales, Louvain.

1961: *Capital in the American Economy.* National Bureau of Economic Research, Princeton, 1961.

1963: 'Notes on the Take-Off', in W. W. Rostow (ed.): *The Economics of Take-Off into Sustained Growth.* Macmillan, London.

LANDES, D. 1949: 'French Entrepreneurship and Industrial Growth in the Nineteenth Century'. *J.E.H.* IX.

1951: 'French Business and Businessmen: A Social and Cultural Analysis' in E. M. Earle (ed.): *Modern France.* Princeton University Press, Princeton, 1951.

1954: 'Social Attitudes, Entrepreneurship, and Economic Development'. *E.E.H.* VI.

1969: *The Unbound Prometheus: Technological Change and Industrial Development in Western Europe from 1750 to the Present Day.* Cambridge University Press, Cambridge.

LEIBENSTEIN, H. 1966a: 'What Can We Expect from a Theory of Development?' *Kyklos* XIX.

1966b: 'Allocative Efficiency versus X Efficiency'. *A.E.R.* LVI.

LEWIS, W. A. 1955: *The Theory of Economic Growth.* Allen and Unwin, London.

LINTON, R. 1952: 'Cultural and Personality Factors Affecting Growth', in B. F. Hoselitz (ed.): *The Progress of Underdeveloped Areas.* Chicago University Press, Chicago.

MCCLELLAND, D. C. 1961: *The Achieving Society.* Van Nostrand, Princeton.

MCCLELLAND, D. C. and WINTER, D. G. 1969: *Motivating Economic Growth.* Free Press, New York.

MCCLOY, S. T. 1952: *French Inventions of the Eighteenth Century.* University of Kentucky Press, Lexington.

MCKENDRICK, N. 1959–60: 'Josiah Wedgwood: An Eighteenth-Century Entrepreneur in Salesmanship and Marketing Techniques'. *E.H.R.* (2) XII.

MCKEOWN, T. and BROWN, R. G. 1955: 'Medical Evidence Related to English Population Changes in the Eighteenth Century'. *Population Studies* IX.

MCKEOWN, T. and RECORD, R. G. 1962–3: 'Reasons for the Decline of Mortality in England and Wales During the Nineteenth Century'. *Population Studies* XVI.

MCLACHLAN, H. 1931: *English Education Under the Test Acts.* Manchester University Press, Manchester.

MANTOUX, P. 1961: *The Industrial Revolution in the Eighteenth Century* (rev'd edn.). Jonathan Cape, London.

MARSHALL, B. 1967: *Capitalism and Nationalism in Prewar Japan: The Ideology of the Business Elite 1868–1941.* Stanford University Press, Stanford.

MARSHALL, T. H. 1929: 'The Population Problem during the Industrial Revolution: A Note on the Present State of the Controversy'. *E.H.*; reprinted in E. M. Carus-Wilson (ed.) 1954: *Essays in Economic History* (Vol. I). Edward Arnold, London.

1929–30: 'Jethro Tull and the "New Husbandry" of the Eighteenth Century'. *E.H.R.* II.

MARTIN, KURT and KNAPP, JOHN, 1967: *The Teaching of Development Economics.* Frank Cass, London.

MATHIAS, P. 1952–3: 'Agriculture and the Brewing and Distilling Industries in the Eighteenth Century'. *E.H.R.* (2) V.

1957–8: 'The Social Structure in the Eighteenth Century: A Calculation by Joseph Massie'. *E.H.R.* (2) X.

1959: *The Brewing Industry in England 1700–1830.* Cambridge University Press, Cambridge.

1969a: *The First Industrial Nation.* Methuen, London.

1969b: 'Who Unbound Prometheus? Science and Technological Change 1600–1800'. *Yorkshire Bulletin of Economic and Social Research* XXI.

MEREDITH, H. O. 1958: *Economic History of England* (6th edn.). Pitman, London.

MERRITT, J. E. 1960: 'The Triangular Trade'. *Business History* III.

MERTON, R. K. 1938: 'Science, Technology and Society in Seventeenth-Century England'. *Osiris* IV.

1961: 'The Role of Genius in Scientific Advance'. *New Scientist* XII.

MILLIKAN, M. F. and BLACKMER, D. L. M. (eds.) 1961: *The Emerging Nations*. Little, Brown Co., Boston.

MINCHINTON, W. E. (ed.) 1968: *Essays in Agrarian History* (2 vols.). A. M. Kelley, New York.

(ed.) 1969: *The Growth of English Overseas Trade in the Seventeenth and Eighteenth Centuries*. Methuen, London.

MINGAY, G. E. 1955–6: 'The Agricultural Depression 1730–1750'. *E.H.R.* (2) VIII; reprinted in E. M. Carus-Wilson (ed.) 1962: *Essays in Economic History* (Vol. II). Edward Arnold, London.

1961–2: 'The Size of Farms in the Eighteenth Century'. *E.H.R.* (2) XIV.

1963a: 'The "Agricultural Revolution" in English History: A Reconsideration'. *Agric. Hist.* XXXVII; reprinted in W. E. Minchinton (ed.) 1968: *Essays in Agrarian History* (Vol. II). David and Charles, Newton Abbot.

1963b: *English Landed Society in the Eighteenth Century*. Routledge and Kegan Paul, London.

1964–5: 'The Land Tax Assessments and the Small Landowner'. *E.H.R.* (2) XVII.

1968: *Enclosure and the Small Farmer in the Age of the Industrial Revolution*. Macmillan, London.

1969: 'Dr Kerridge's "Agricultural Revolution": A Comment'. *Agric. Hist.* XLIII.

MITCHELL, B. R. and DEANE, PHYLLIS, 1962: *Abstract of British Historical Statistics*. Cambridge University Press, Cambridge.

MOFFIT, L. W. 1963: *England on the Eve of the Industrial Revolution*. Frank Cass, London.

MOORE, W. E. 1951: *Industrialization and Labour: Social Aspects of Economic Development*. Cornell University Press, Ithaca.

1955: 'Labour Attitudes Towards Industrialization in Underdeveloped Countries'. *A.E.R.* Supplement XLV.

MORGAN, E. V. 1939: 'Some Aspects of the Bank Restriction Period 1797–1821'. *E.H.* III.

MORGAN, J. N. 1963-4: 'The Achievement Motive and Economic Behaviour'. *E.D.C.C.* XII.

MUSSON, A. E. 1957-8: 'James Nasmyth and the Early Growth of Mechanical Engineering'. *E.H.R.* (2) X.

MUSSON, A. E. and ROBINSON, E. 1958-9: 'The Early Growth of Steam Power', *E.H.R.* (2) XI.

1960-61: 'Science and Industry in the Late Eighteenth Century'. *E.H.R.* (2) XIII.

1969: *Science and Technology in the Industrial Revolution*. Manchester University Press, Manchester.

MYA MAUNG, 1964: 'Cultural Values and Economic Change in Burma'. *Asian Survey* IV.

MYINT, H. 1965: 'Education and Economic Development'. *Social and Economic Studies* XIV.

NEEDHAM, J. 1964: 'Science and Society in East and West'. *Science and Society* XXVIII.

1969: *The Grand Titration: Science and Society in East and West*. Allen and Unwin, London.

NEF, J. U. 1932: *The Rise of the British Coal Industry*. Frank Cass, London.

1934: 'The Progress of Technology and the Growth of Large-scale Industry in Great Britain, 1540-1640'. *E.H.R.* V; reprinted in E. M. Carus-Wilson (ed.) 1954: *Essays in Economic History* (Vol. I). Edward Arnold, London.

1937: 'Prices and Industrial Capitalism in France and England 1540-1640'. *E.H.R.* VII.

1940: *Industry and Government in France and England 1540-1640*. American Philosophical Association, Memoirs.

1943: 'The Industrial Revolution Reconsidered'. *J.E.H.* III.

1950: 'The Industrial Revolution Reconsidered', in *War and Human Progress*. Routledge and Kegan Paul, London.

OGILVIE, SIR C. 1958: *The King's Government and the Common Law 1471-1641*. Blackwell, Oxford.

OHKAWA, K. and ROSOVSKY, H. 1960: 'The Role of Agriculture in Modern Japanese Economic Development'. *E.D.C.C.* IX.

ORENSTEIN, H. 1963: 'Village, Caste, and the Welfare State'. *H.O.* XXII.

ORWIN, C. S. 1933: 'Agriculture and Rural Life', in A. S. Turberville (ed.): *Johnson's England* (Vol. I). Clarendon Press, Oxford.

1952: *A History of English Farming*. Nelson, London.

ORWIN, C. S. and ORWIN, C. S. 1954: *The Open Fields* (2nd edn.). Clarendon Press, Oxford.

PARKER, R. A. C. 1955-6: 'Coke of Norfolk and the Agrarian Revolution'. *E.H.R.* (2) VIII.

PARKINSON, C. N. (ed.) 1948: *The Trade Winds: A Study of British*

Overseas Trade During the French Wars, 1793–1815. Allen and Unwin, London.

PARSONS, TALCOTT, 1958: 'Institutional Framework of Economic Development', in *The Challenge of Economic Development*. Eliezer Kaplan School of Economics and Social Sciences, The Hebrew University, Jerusalem.

Peacock, J. L. 1969: 'Religion, Communications, and Modernization: A Weberian Critique of Some Recent Views'. *H.O.* XXVIII.

PEASLEE, A. 1968–9: 'Education's Role in Development'. *E.D.C.C.* XVII.

PERKIN, H. J. 1968: 'The Social Causes of the Industrial Revolution'. *Transactions of the Royal Historical Society* 5th series, XVIII.

POLLARD, S. 1958–9: 'Investment, Consumption and the Industrial Revolution'. *E.H.R.* (2) XI.

1963: 'Capital Accounting in the Industrial Revolution'. *Yorkshire Bulletin of Economic and Social Research* XV.

1963–4: 'Factory Discipline in the Industrial Revolution'. *E.H.R.* (2) XVI.

1964a: 'The Factory Village in the Industrial Revolution'. *English Historical Review* LXXIX.

1964b: 'Fixed Capital in the Industrial Revolution in Britain'. *J.E.H.* XXIV.

1965: *The Genesis of Modern Management*. Edward Arnold, London (reprinted 1968 by Penguin, London).

1968a: 'The Growth and Distribution of Capital in Great Britain, c. 1770–1870', in *Third International Conference of Economic History*. Moulton, Paris.

1968b: *The Idea of Progress: History and Society*. Watts, London.

POLLARD, S. and HOLMES, C. 1968: *Documents of European Economic History*: Vol. I, *The Process of Industrialization 1750–1870*. Edward Arnold, London.

POSTAN, M. M. 1935–6: 'Recent Trends in the Accumulation of Capital'. *E.H.R.* VI.

POTTER, J. 1960: 'Atlantic Economy, 1815–60: the U.S.A. and the Industrial Revolution in Britain', in L. S. Pressnell (ed.): *Studies in the Industrial Revolution*. University of London, London.

1962: ' "Optimism" and "Pessimism" in Interpreting the Industrial Revolution: An Economic Historian's Dilemma'. *Scandinavian Economic History Review* X.

PRESSNELL, L. S. 1952–3: 'Public Monies and the Development of English Banking'. *E.H.R.* (2) V.

1956: *Country Banking in the Industrial Revolution*. Clarendon Press, Oxford.

1960: 'The Rate of Interest in the Eighteenth Century', in L. S.

Pressnell (ed.): *Studies in the Industrial Revolution*. University of London, London.

QUINT, M. 1958: 'The Idea of Progress in an Iraqi Village'. *Middle East Journal* XII.

RAISTRICK, A. 1950: *Quakers in Science and Industry*. Bannisdale Press, London.

1953: *Dynasty of Iron Founders: The Darbys and Coalbrookdale*. Longmans, Green, London.

RAMSAY, G. D. 1957: *English Overseas Trade during the Centuries of Emergence*. Macmillan, London.

RANIS, G. 1955: 'The Community-Centred Entrepreneur in Japanese Development'. *E.E.H.* VIII.

RAZZELL, P. E. 1965: 'Population Change in Eighteenth-Century England: A reinterpretation'. *E.H.R.* (*2*) XVIII.

REDFORD, A. 1964: *Labour Migration in England 1800–1850* (2nd edn.). Manchester University Press, Manchester.

REDLICH, F. 1957–8: 'Business Leadership: Diverse Origins and Variant Forms'. *E.D.C.C.* VI.

RICHES, N. 1967: *The Agricultural Revolution in Norfolk* (2nd edn.). Frank Cass, London.

ROBERTSON, H. M. 1959: *Aspects of the Rise of Economic Individualism*. Kelley and Millman, New York.

ROBERTSON, M. L. 1956–7: 'Scottish Commerce and the American War of Independence'. *E.H.R.* (*2*) IX.

ROBINSON, E. 1956 and 1957: 'The Lunar Society and the Improvement of Scientific Instruments'. *Annals of Science* XII and XIII.

1963–4: 'Eighteenth-Century Commerce and Fashion: Matthew Boulton's Marketing Techniques'. *E.H.R.* (*2*) XVI.

ROBINSON, E. A. G. 1954: 'The Changing Structure of the British Economy'. *E.J.* LXIV.

ROSOVSKY, H. (ed.) 1966: *Industrialization in Two Systems*. Wiley, New York.

ROSTOW, W. W. 1955: 'Trends in the Allocation of Resources in Secular Growth', in L. H. Dupriez (ed.) *Economic Progress*. Institut de Recherches Economiques et Sociales, Louvain.

1960: *The Stages of Economic Growth*. Cambridge University Press, Cambridge.

(ed.) 1963a: *The Economics of Take-Off into Sustained Growth*. Macmillan, London.

1963b: 'Leading Sectors in the Take-Off', in W. W. Rostow (ed.): *The Economics of Take-Off into Sustained Growth*. Macmillan, London.

SALTER, W. E. G. 1960: *Productivity and Technical Change.* Cambridge University Press, Cambridge.

SAMUELSSON, K. 1961: *Religion and Economic Action* (translated by E. Geoffrey French). Heinemann, London.

SAWYER, J. E. 1951: 'Strains in the Social Structure of Modern France', in Edward M. Earle (ed.): *Modern France.* Princeton University Press, Princeton.

1962: 'The Entrepreneur and the Social Order: France and the United States', in William Miller (ed.): *Men in Business* (rev'd. edn.). Harper and Row, New York.

SCHLOTE, W. 1952: *British Overseas Trade from 1700 to the 1930s.* Blackwell, Oxford.

SCHMOOKLER, J. 1962: 'Economic Sources of Inventive Activity'. *J.E.H.* XXII.

1966: *Invention and Economic Growth.* Harvard University Press, Cambridge, Mass.

SCHOFIELD, R. E. 1953: 'John Wesley and Science in Eighteenth-Century England'. *Isis* XLIV.

1956: 'Josiah Wedgwood and a Proposed Eighteenth-Century Industrial Research Organization'. *Isis* XLVII.

1957: 'The Industrial Orientation of Science in the Lunar Society of Birmingham'. *Isis* XLVIII.

1963: *The Lunar Society of Birmingham: A Social History of Provincial Science and Industry in Eighteenth-Century England.* Clarendon Press, Oxford.

SCHULTZ, T. W. 1964: *Transforming Traditional Agriculture.* Yale University Press, New Haven.

1968: *Economic Growth and Agriculture.* McGraw-Hill, New York.

SCHUMPETER, E. 1960: *English Overseas Trade Statistics 1697–1808.* Clarendon Press, Oxford.

SHANNON, H. A. 1931: 'The Coming of General Limited Liability'. *E.H.* II.

SHAPIRO, SEYMOUR, 1967: *Capital and the Cotton Industry in the Industrial Revolution.* Cornell University Press, Ithaca.

SHERIDAN, R. B. 1958–9: 'The Commercial and Financial Organization of the British Slave Trade, 1750–1807'. *E.H.R.* (2) XI.

SIMON, B. 1960: *Studies in the History of Education 1780–1870.* Lawrence and Wishart, London.

SINGER, C. S. *et al.* (eds.) 1954–8: *A History of Technology.* Clarendon Press, Oxford.

SINGER, M. 1965–6: 'Religion and Social Change in India: The Max Weber Thesis, Phase Three'. *E.D.C.C.* XIV.

SMELSER, N. J. 1959: *Social Change in the Industrial Revolution: An*

Application of Theory to the Lancashire Cotton Industry 1770–1840. Routledge and Kegan Paul, London.

1963: *The Sociology of Economic Life.* Prentice-Hall, Englewood Cliffs, New Jersey.

SMITH, THOMAS C. 1959: *The Agrarian Origins of Modern Japan.* Stanford University Press, Stanford, California.

SMITHIES, A. 1961: 'Rising Expectations and Economic Development'. *E.J.* LXXI.

SOLTOW, J. 1968: 'The Entrepreneur in Economic History'. *A.E.R.* Supplement LVIII.

SPENGLER, J. J. 1968: 'Demographic Factors and Early Modern Economic Development'. *Daedalus* XCVII.

STONE, L. 1964: 'The Educational Revolution in England, 1560–1640'. *Past and Present* XXVIII.

1969: 'Literacy and Education in England, 1640–1900'. *Past and Present* XLII.

SULLIVAN, J. W. N. 1928: *The Bases of Modern Science.* Ernest Benn, London.

SUPPLE, B. E. 1961: 'Economic History and Economic Underdevelopment'. *C.J.E.P.* XXVII.

TATE, W. E. 1945: 'Opposition to Parliamentary Enclosure in the Eighteenth Century'. *Agric. Hist.* XIX.

TAWNEY, A. J. and TAWNEY, R. H. 1934–5: 'An Occupational Census of the Seventeenth Century'. *E.H.R.* V.

TAWNEY, R. H. 1912: *The Agrarian Problem in the Sixteenth Century.* Longmans, London.

1926: *Religion and the Rise of Capitalism;* 2nd edn. 1937, reprinted 1969 by Penguin, London.

TAYLOR, A. J. 1960: 'Progress and Poverty in Britain, 1780–1850: A Reappraisal'. *History* XLV; reprinted in E. M. Carus-Wilson (ed.) 1962: *Essays in Economic History* (Vol. III). Edward Arnold, London.

THIRSK, J. 1957: *English Peasant Farming.* Routledge and Kegan Paul, London.

1959: *Tudor Enclosures.* Historical Association Pamphlet, General Series, No. 41.

1961: 'Industries in the Countryside' in F. J. Fisher (ed.): *Essays in the Economic and Social History of Tudor and Stuart England.* Cambridge University Press, Cambridge.

1970: 'Seventeenth-Century Agriculture and Social Change'. *A.H.R.* XVIII Supplement.

THOMPSON, A. G. 1966: 'History to Scale? The British Economy in the Eighteenth Century: A Comment'. *Business Archives and History* VI.

THOMPSON, E. P. 1963: *The Making of the English Working Class.* Gollancz, London.

TREVOR-ROPER, H. 1967: *Religion, the Reformation and Social Change, and other essays.* Macmillan, London.

TROW-SMITH, R. 1951: *English Husbandry, from the Earliest Times to the Present Day.* Faber and Faber, London.

  1957: *A History of British Livestock Husbandry 1700–1900.* Routledge and Kegan Paul, London.

TRUPP, S. L. 1941: 'Social Control in the Medieval Town.' *J.E.H* Supplement.

TUCKER, G. S. L. 1963: 'English Pre-Industrial Population Trends'. *E.H.R.* (2) XVI.

UBBELOHDE, A. R. J. P. 1958: 'The Beginning of the Change from Craft Mystery to Science as a Basis for Technology', in C. Singer *et al.* (eds.): *A History of Technology* (Vol. IV). Clarendon Press, Oxford.

U.S. DEPARTMENT OF COMMERCE, 1949: *Historical Statistics of the United States 1789–1945.* Bureau of Census, Washington.

USHER, A. P. 1954: *A History of Mechanical Inventions* (rev'd edn.). Harvard University Press, Cambridge, Mass.

WADSWORTH, A. P. and MANN, J. DE L. 1931: *The Cotton Trade and Industrial Lancashire 1600–1780.* Manchester University Press, Manchester.

WARNER, R. S. 1970: 'The Role of Religious Ideas and the Use of Models in Max Weber's Comparative Studies of Non-Capitalist Societies'. *J.E.H.* XXX.

WARNER, W. J. 1967: *The Wesleyan Movement in the Industrial Revolution.* Russell and Russell, New York.

WEBER, MAX, 1930: *The Protestant Ethic and the Spirit of Capitalism.* Allen and Unwin, London.

WEINER, MYRON (ed.) 1966: *Modernization: The Dynamics of Growth.* Basic Books, New York.

WERTIME, THEO, 1962: *The Coming of the Age of Steel.* University of Chicago Press, Chicago.

WESLEY, J. 1872: *The Works of John Wesley* (14 vols.). Wesleyan Conference Office, London.

WEST, E. G. 1970: 'Resource Allocation and Growth in Early Nineteenth Century British Education'. *E.H.R.* (2) XXIII.

  1971: 'The Interpretation of Early Nineteenth-Century Education Statistics'. *E.H.R.* (2) XXIV.

WESTFALL, R. S. 1956: 'Unpublished Boyle Papers Relating to Scientific Method'. *Annals of Science* XII.

WHITE, L. J. 1969: 'Enclosures and Population Movements in England 1700–1830'. *E.E.H.* 2nd series, VI.

WHITEHEAD, D. 1964: 'History to Scale? The British Economy in the Eighteenth Century'. *Business Archives and History* IV.

WILSON, C. 1941: *Anglo-Dutch Commerce and Finance in the Eighteenth Century*, Cambridge University Press, Cambridge.

1955: 'The Entrepreneur in the Industrial Revolution in Britain'. *E.E.H.* VII; reprinted in B. Supple (ed.) 1963: *The Experience of Economic Growth*. Random House, New York.

1965: *England's Apprenticeship 1603–1763*. Longmans, London.

WILSON, C. and CARTER, A. 1959–60: 'Dutch Investment in Eighteenth-century England'. *E.H.R.* (2) XII.

WILSON, R. G. 1966: 'Transport Dues as Indices of Economic Growth 1775–1820'. *E.H.R.* XIX.

WOODRUFF, W. 1956: 'Capitalism and the Historians: A Contribution to the Discussion on the Industrial Revolution'. *J.E.H.* XVI.

WRIGLEY, E. A. 1966a: 'Family Limitation in Pre-Industrial England'. *E.H.R.* (2) XIX.

(ed.) 1966b: *An Introduction to English Historical Demography, from the Sixteenth to the Nineteenth Century*. Weidenfeld and Nicolson, London.

1967: 'A Simple Model of London's Importance in Changing English Society and Economy 1650–1750'. *Past and Present* XXXVII.

1969: *Population and History*. Weidenfeld and Nicolson.

1970: Population, Family and Household', in Martin Ballard (ed.): *New Movements in the Study and Teaching of History*. Temple Smith, London.

Index